AF264335

AI AT WAR

A Double-Edged Sword

JUSTIN K. KOJOK

Books By Justin K. Kojok

NOVELS

- DRIVING FOR JUSTICE
- WHISPERS IN THE VINEYARD

NONFICTION

- INTERCESSOR: A COLLECTION OF MY FERVENT PRAYERS
- CYBERSECURITY: SAFEGUARDING OUR DIGITAL WORLD
- MOTIVATIONAL ANDF INSPIRATIONAL QUOTES

PLEASE SCAN THIS QR CODE TO BUY THESE BOOKS.

AI AT WAR

A DOUBLE-EDGED SWORD

Global Impact Press, LLC

Copyright © 2026 By Justin K. Kojok
AI AT WAR: A Double-Edged Sword

Publisher: Global Impact Press, LLC

Contact: author@globalimpactpress.com
Website: https://globalimpactpress.com
Interior and Cover design: J.K. Designs, USA

Printed Worldwide
First Printing 2026
First Edition 2026

ISBN: 978-1-966348-10-8 (Hardcover)
ISBN: 978-1-966348-09-2 (Paperback)
ISBN: 978-1-966348-11-5 (eBook)

Library of Congress Control Number 2026910406

Disclaimer Notice:
Please note the information contained within this book is for educational purposes only. All effort has been made to present accurate, up to date, and reliable, complete information.
The content within this book has been derived from various sources.
By reading this book, the reader agrees that under no circumstances is the author responsible for any losses, direct or indirect, which are incurred as a result of the use of information contained within book, including, but not limited to, errors, omissions or inaccuracies.

To my late father, Kojok Kalipang, you read no books

but you taught me everything worth knowing.

This one is for you.

<u>CONTENTS</u>

INTRODUCTION
THE SWORD THAT CUTS BOTH WAYS

The whole thing began, as so many modern catastrophes do, without a single human adversary pressing a single key.

In August 2025, the production lines at Jaguar Land Rover went silent. Not all at once, and not with the dramatic bang of an explosion or the obvious theatre of a ransom note splashed across every monitor. The silence crept in through the supply chain, spreading upstream and downstream through a web of more than 5,000 interconnected suppliers, each trusting the next, each assuming the digital handshakes passing between them were exactly what they seemed. By the time the scope of the intrusion became clear, five weeks of global production had been lost. The direct cost approached £200 million. The broader ripple effect through the British automotive supply chain, according to subsequent analyses reported in the wake of the World Economic Forum's Global Cybersecurity Outlook 2026, reached nearly two billion pounds when every disrupted component delivery, idled factory floor, and shattered logistics contract was tallied. Five thousand suppliers. Billions in damage. And at the center of it all, not a team of elite hackers hunched over keyboards in some shadowed server room, but an adversary that had learned to move with patience, precision, and machine-assisted speed, exploiting the blind spots between trusted relationships rather than battering through fortified walls. That incident was not an anomaly. It was a signal.

Two months earlier, in April 2025, a Norwegian hydroelectric dam had been deliberately sabotaged through a cyber intrusion that opened a floodgate, releasing 500 liters of water per second for four continuous hours. Across Europe, hybrid attacks combining cyber intrusions with drone strikes and coordinated disinformation campaigns had targeted airports and critical infrastructure. Nation-state actors, primarily linked to Russia, had spent months quietly tunneling through American telecommunications networks, their presence discovered only in retrospect. And in corporate boardrooms from London to Singapore to São Paulo, executives were receiving video calls from the voices and faces of their own CFOs, COOs, and legal counsel, compelling fund transfers, contract signatures, and credential disclosures, before anyone realized the person on the screen had never existed at all. The voice was synthesized. The face was rendered. The damage was real.

Welcome to 2026, and to the age of the AI-powered cyberwar.

The Convergence We Did Not Fully Anticipate

There is a kind of technological reckoning that arrives not as a sudden rupture but as the accumulation of a thousand smaller shifts, each one manageable in isolation, collectively transformative. The convergence of artificial intelligence and cybersecurity is exactly that kind of reckoning.

For years, security professionals operated in a world of known quantities. Attackers developed malware; defenders built signatures to catch it. Attackers probed for vulnerabilities; defenders patched them. Attackers sent phishing emails; defenders trained employees to recognize the telltale grammatical awkwardness, the mismatched sender domain, and the suspicious link. The arms race was real and relentless, but its tempo was, broadly speaking, human. Human attackers planning human intrusions against human defenders making human decisions. There were tools on both sides, of course, increasingly sophisticated ones, but the underlying rhythm of the conflict remained tied to the pace at which people could think, decide, and act. That rhythm is gone.

According to the CrowdStrike 2026 Global Threat Report, the average eCrime breakout time, the critical window between an attacker's initial foothold and their lateral movement to other high-value systems, fell to just twenty-nine minutes in 2025, a sixty-five percent increase in speed from the year before. The fastest observed breakout in that period took twenty-seven seconds. In one documented intrusion, data exfiltration began within four minutes of initial access. These are not the timelines of human planning. These are the execution timelines for the machine.

The World Economic Forum's Global Cybersecurity Outlook 2026, drawing on responses from over eight hundred leaders across ninety-two countries, found that ninety-four percent of respondents expect AI to be the most significant driver of change in cybersecurity this year, while eighty-seven percent identified AI-related vulnerabilities as the fastest-growing cyber risk they experienced across 2025. These figures are not the projections of researchers speculating about a distant future. They are the assessments of the CISOs, CEOs, and security executives who are living inside this war right now.

What makes 2026 genuinely pivotal, rather than merely another year of escalating threat statistics, is not any single attack or innovation. It is the simultaneous maturation of several intersecting forces that are reshaping the entire geometry of digital conflict. Generative AI has moved from novelty to weapon, from productivity tool to attack platform, used by adversaries to craft hyper-personalized phishing campaigns at an industrial scale, generate polymorphic malware that rewrites its own code to evade detection, and produce synthetic media so convincing that human discernment has effectively ceased to be a reliable last line of defense. Agentic AI, systems capable of taking autonomous sequences of action without constant human instruction, has introduced an entirely new class of attack surface into the enterprise, as organizations rush to deploy AI agents for everything from customer service to code review without the governance frameworks to secure them. And on the defensive side, AI has become not merely useful but necessary, the only technology capable of operating at the speed and scale required to match an adversary that no longer needs to sleep.

This is the double-edged sword at the heart of this book.

The Sword Metaphor, and Why It Matters

The sword cuts both ways. Every capability that AI delivers to an attacker has a corresponding, if not always symmetrical, defensive application. The same large language model that enables a threat actor to generate thousands of perfectly localized spear-phishing emails, each one indistinguishable from authentic correspondence from a trusted colleague, also enables a defender to analyze behavioral patterns across millions of network events and surface anomalies that no human analyst could detect in time. The same agentic AI framework that allows an adversary to automate reconnaissance, credential theft, and lateral movement across a compromised environment also allows a security operations center to automate triage, prioritize alerts, and execute containment responses in seconds rather than hours.

But the sword metaphor carries a warning. A sword in the hands of someone who does not know how to wield it is more dangerous to its owner than to any opponent. And right now, in the asymmetric reality of the 2026 threat landscape, the attackers have spent more time mastering the blade. AI-enabled adversaries increased their operations by eighty-nine percent year-over-year in 2025, weaponizing AI across reconnaissance, credential theft, and evasion, with intrusions moving through trusted identities, SaaS applications, and cloud infrastructure while blending into normal activity. Meanwhile, the organizations charged with defending against these attacks are still, in many cases, deploying AI tools without the governance structures, the security assessments, or the institutional knowledge to understand what they have introduced into their environments.

More than one-third of organizations still deploy AI tools without checking whether they are secure, racing to adopt the latest technology without fully understanding the risks they are importing alongside the efficiency gains. The sword, in those cases, cuts inward.

This book is about understanding the blade: what it can do, what it has already done, who is wielding it and how, and what it will take to use it wisely in defense of the systems and institutions that underpin modern civilization.

What This Book Is, and What It Is Not

AI at War is not a technical manual. It does not require its reader to possess a background in machine learning, network architecture, or penetration testing. It is written for the executives who understand that their company's most significant risk in 2026 sits at the intersection of AI adoption and security governance, but who needs a clear-eyed account of why, grounded in current evidence, before they can act. It is written for the security practitioners who live inside this war daily but want the broader strategic and geopolitical context that rarely makes it into threat feeds. It is written for the students, the policymakers, the journalists, the board members, and the informed citizens who suspect, correctly, that what happens in the cyber domain over the next several years will shape the physical world in ways most people are not yet prepared to reckon with.

The approach throughout this book is narrative. Each chapter opens with a story, an incident, a moment in which the abstract becomes concrete, and the statistics behind a threat become the experience of a specific person or organization that encountered it. The anecdotes are drawn from documented cases; the statistics and analytical frameworks are sourced from the 2025 and 2026 reports of the world's leading cybersecurity intelligence organizations, including the World Economic Forum, CrowdStrike, IBM X-Force, Darktrace, Palo Alto Networks, and NIST, among others. Where expert analysis is paraphrased, its origin is noted. Nothing here is invented.

A Roadmap Through the War

This book unfolds in four broad movements. The first, covering Chapters One through Three, establishes the battlefield. Chapter One traces the historical convergence of AI and cybersecurity, from early machine learning applications in intrusion detection through the generative AI explosion that redrew the threat map after 2022. Chapter Two catalogs the new arsenal of adversaries: the specific ways in which AI has transformed the attacker's toolkit, from deepfake-enabled social engineering and polymorphic malware to AI-orchestrated supply-chain intrusions and the autonomous agents now conducting reconnaissance on corporate infrastructure. Chapter Three examines the defensive response: the AI-powered detection, behavioral analytics, and automated response systems that organizations such as Darktrace, SentinelOne, and CrowdStrike have deployed to keep pace with machine-accelerated attacks.

The second movement, Chapters Four through Six, turns the lens inward, examining AI itself as a target and a terrain. Chapter Four confronts the attack surface of intelligent systems: prompt injection, data poisoning, model inversion, adversarial inputs, and the supply-chain risks embedded in the training data and open-source model repositories on which the entire AI ecosystem depends. Chapter Five explores the specific dynamics of generative AI in the cyber trenches, including both its exploitation by attackers and the emerging defensive tools, such as watermarking and synthetic data generation, being developed to counter it. Chapter Six addresses one of the most consequential and underappreciated problems of the agentic era: what happens to identity and access management when the entity requesting permissions is not a human but an autonomous AI agent capable of making decisions that no human explicitly authorized.

The third movement, Chapters Seven through Ten, situates the technical conflict within its broader contexts. Chapter Seven maps the 2026 ecosystem of vendors, platforms, and open-source tools available to practitioners. Chapter Eight examines the geopolitical, regulatory, and ethical dimensions of AI-enabled cyber conflict, including the EU AI Act's implications, the evolving NIST Cyber AI Profile, and the state-sponsored operations that have made sovereign AI infrastructure a matter of national security. Chapter Nine presents detailed case studies of real-world deployments and breaches from 2025 and 2026, tracing the specific decisions and gaps that determined outcomes. Chapter Ten distills practical strategic guidance for organizations navigating this landscape, from AI security assessments and Zero Trust architecture to red-teaming AI systems and building governance frameworks that can keep pace with adoption.

The book's final movement, Chapters Eleven and Twelve, together with a closing Conclusion, projects the trajectory forward. What does the threat landscape look like when agentic AI systems are no longer experimental but operational infrastructure? What happens when quantum computing capabilities begin intersecting with

AI-powered attacks? And what does it mean, practically and ethically, to build resilience in a world where the adversary is increasingly a machine, and the defender must become one too?

The Stakes

IBM CEO Arvind Krishna, writing in the World Economic Forum's 2026 Cybersecurity Outlook, put the challenge plainly, 'Those who defend the digital world must use every tool at their disposal, which now includes agentic AI, because the criminals already are." As the World Economic Forum report frames it, the result is a fast-paced, metamorphic landscape where disruptions move swiftly across borders, even as technology offers new potential for resilience.

But resilience is not passive or automatic. The World Economic Forum's research warns explicitly that AI is accelerating cybersecurity risks at unprecedented speed, and that the gap between organizations that have built the governance, visibility, and collaborative infrastructure to absorb shocks and those that have not, will continue to widen.

That gap is where this book lives. The organizations on the right side of it have not merely acquired better tools. They have developed a fundamentally different relationship with both risk and technology, one that treats cyber resilience not as a cost center or a compliance checkbox but as a strategic capability, a competitive advantage, and in some cases, a matter of survival.

The sword is already in play. The question is who learns to wield it first, and wisely.

Let's begin.

"A sword in the hands of someone who does not know how to wield it is more dangerous to its owner than to any opponent." - JK Kojok.

CHAPTER 1

THE CONVERGENCE

The signature-based security model of the late 1990s and early 2000s was always fighting the last war. Detection systems matched incoming traffic against catalogues of known-bad patterns; when attackers used techniques outside those catalogues, the systems were blind. Researchers had been building intrusion detection systems since Dorothy Denning's foundational 1987 paper, and by 1998, DARPA had called for systematic research into machine learning methods for security. The ambition was present. What was missing were three things that had not yet fully arrived: sufficient data, adequate computing power, and the algorithmic maturity to turn raw network telemetry into something resembling intelligence.

For roughly a decade and a half, the field lived in that tension. Attackers, unconstrained by the need to stay inside any predefined catalogue of behaviors, innovated freely. Defenders updated their signature databases, patched their systems, and hoped that nothing genuinely novel arrived before the next vendor update. They rarely did.

Then, gradually and then suddenly, the conditions changed.

The Big Data Inflection and the Rise of Behavioral Intelligence

The early 2000s and 2010s marked a transformative period, with machine learning emerging as a pivotal force as the internet became ubiquitous and data volume grew exponentially. Every transaction, every login, and every packet traversing the network left a trace. Where there were traces, there were patterns. And where there were patterns, there were machines that could learn them.

In the late 2000s, supervised learning algorithms paved the way for more accurate threat detection and prevention. Unsupervised learning algorithms followed, enabling the identification of anomalous patterns and previously unknown threats. The rise of deep learning in the 2010s revolutionized cybersecurity by enabling the processing of vast amounts of data and the discovery of complex patterns, while natural language processing techniques gained prominence for enhanced analysis of textual data and the detection of social engineering attacks.

This shift from signature-based to behavior-based detection was not merely a technical upgrade. It represented a philosophical reorientation of the entire defensive enterprise. The old model asked: "Does this match something we know is bad?" The new model asked: "Does this deviate from what we know is normal?" The distinction sounds subtle. Its operational consequences were enormous.

Consider what behavioral anomaly detection essentially means in practice. An enterprise deploys an ML-powered security platform that spends weeks establishing baselines: this user typically logs in from London between eight in the morning and six in the evening, accesses these file shares, uses these applications, and generates this pattern of network traffic. When, one Thursday at two in the morning, a login emerges from a data center in Eastern Europe and immediately begins querying the financial records database, the system does not need a signature for "suspicious activity from Eastern Europe at 2 a.m." It knows the behavior is anomalous. It flags it. In some architectures, it blocks it automatically and summons an analyst before the attacker has had time to pivot.

AI establishes a baseline of normal behavior for users, devices, and applications, enabling the detection of anomalies: any deviation, such as a user who typically accesses marketing documents suddenly attempting to download financial data, is flagged as a potential threat. Threat hunting became proactive rather than reactive. Security teams began moving from a posture of detection after damage to one of anticipation, using historical telemetry to model attacker behavior and hunt for early indicators of compromise before a breach fully materializes.

By the mid-2010s, the major commercial security vendors had largely internalized this shift. Endpoint detection and response platforms began integrating ML-driven behavioral analysis alongside traditional signature scanning. Network traffic analysis tools learned to identify command-and-control communications even when they used encryption or mimicked legitimate protocols. User and entity behavior analytics platforms emerged, correlating identity signals across authentication logs, application usage, and data access to build remarkably granular portraits of what "normal" looked like for every human and system in an environment. Security information and event management platforms began applying machine learning to the problem of alert correlation, helping overwhelmed analysts separate the genuine emergencies from the noise.

The defensive application of machine learning in cybersecurity, in other words, was well underway before the event that changed everything.

November 2022, and the Door That Swung Open

On November 30, 2022, OpenAI released ChatGPT to the public. Within five days, it had one million users. Within two months, one hundred million. Whatever one thinks of the hyperbole that surrounded the launch, the underlying phenomenon was real and consequential: for the first time, the capabilities of large language models, systems trained on vast corpora of human-generated text to predict and generate language with remarkable fluency, became accessible to anyone with a browser and an internet connection. No technical background required. No API credentials. No knowledge of machine learning. Just a text box, a question, and an answer that arrived in seconds.

The security community recognized the implications almost immediately, and they were double-edged almost from the start.

On the defensive side, large language models offered extraordinary potential for security operations work. Analysts had long been drowning in textual complexity: threat intelligence reports, vulnerability disclosures, malware analysis writeups, incident response logs, and regulatory guidance. LLMs could read and synthesize that material at a speed no human team could approach. They could assist with writing detection rules, explaining code, translating cryptic log entries into plain-language summaries, and generating draft incident reports. Security vendors raced to integrate generative AI capabilities into their platforms. The security operations center with overwhelming cognitive load and punishing alert fatigue, suddenly had a potential force multiplier that could help analysts think, not just react.

On the offensive side, the same accessibility that made LLMs useful for defenders made them dangerous in other hands. Crafting a convincing phishing email had always required a certain investment of effort, particularly when targeting someone in another culture or language. LLMs eliminated that friction. Generating plausible pretexts for social engineering attacks, writing scripts for vishing calls, and producing synthetic business email compromise content that mirrored the authentic voice of a compromised executive, all of it became operationally trivial. The democratization of generative AI capabilities meant that threat actors who had previously been limited by their own technical skills or linguistic resources suddenly had access to a tool that could automatically bridge those gaps.

As the World Economic Forum's Global Cybersecurity Outlook 2026 observed, generative AI's democratization of technology opens a new world of tools and capabilities to people who are not traditional developers or technologists, with significant productivity benefits but also a new range of cybersecurity issues, including that threat actors now have access to AI-enabled tools that can accelerate the discovery and exploitation of potential gaps in an organization's networks.

The door had swung open, and it swung in both directions simultaneously.

The Agentic Inflection: From Tools to Actors

The generative AI wave of 2022 through 2024 was, in retrospect, the prologue. The more consequential shift arrived in 2024 and accelerated dramatically through 2025: the emergence of agentic AI.

The distinction between a generative AI tool and an agentic AI system is not merely technical. It is the difference between a very sophisticated calculator and an autonomous actor. A generative AI tool responds to prompts. It produces text, code, images, and analysis. It waits for input, generates output, and stops. An agentic AI system operates on the basis of goals. Given an objective, it reasons about the steps required to achieve it, selects and uses tools, takes actions in the digital environment, observes the results, adjusts its approach, and continues until the goal is met or it is stopped. It does not wait for the next prompt. It acts.

Generative AI does excellent work when given the right prompt; agentic AI can carry out a project when given a goal. It can assemble the resources, coordinate the work, and pursue the goal autonomously. The implications of this distinction, when applied to the cybersecurity context, are profound and still unfolding.

On the enterprise side, the deployment of AI agents accelerated throughout 2025 as organizations discovered how dramatically they could amplify operational efficiency. AI assistants were wired into ticketing systems, source code repositories, chat platforms, and cloud dashboards. In some environments, these systems could open pull requests, query internal databases, book services, and trigger automated workflows with limited human involvement. A single agent, operating continuously, could accomplish in hours what a human team might take days to complete. The productivity mathematics were compelling enough that adoption frequently outpaced governance.

According to the Cisco State of AI Security 2026 report, organizations granted agentic systems the authority to execute tasks, access databases, and modify code, with many deployments moving forward with limited readiness: only twenty-nine percent of organizations reported being prepared to secure those deployments. The gap between deployment pace and security maturity was, in the language of every breach report ever written, an attack surface.

And attackers noticed. A Dark Reading readership poll found that forty-eight percent of cybersecurity professionals now identify agentic AI and autonomous systems as the top attack vector heading into 2026, outranking deepfake threats, board-level cyber recognition, and passwordless adoption. The finding reflects something that practitioners have been articulating with increasing urgency: AI agents, by design, carry elevated permissions across multiple systems. They have access to databases, code repositories, communication platforms, and external APIs. They operate with minimal human oversight. They rely on the inputs they receive to function. Every one of those characteristics is an attack vector waiting to be exploited, and the architecture of the standard enterprise AI agent was built for functionality rather than adversarial resilience.

Palo Alto Networks, in its 2026 cybersecurity predictions, noted that autonomous agents already outnumber humans in some enterprise environments by an 82-to-1 ratio, creating a trust crisis in which a single forged command can trigger an automated cascade of consequences. The math is vertiginous. If an organization has deployed dozens of AI agents across its operations, each with legitimate access to sensitive systems, and an attacker successfully manipulates even one of those agents through a prompt injection or a poisoned memory entry, the blast radius is not the blast radius of a single compromised endpoint. It is the blast radius of everything that the agent could reach.

The Inseparability Thesis

All this history, from Denning's 1987 intrusion detection model through the DARPA benchmarks of the late 1990s, the behavioral analytics revolution of the 2010s, the generative AI inflection of 2022, and the agentic AI emergence of 2024 and 2025, converges on a single, inescapable thesis: AI and cybersecurity are no longer adjacent fields that occasionally intersect. They are in the same field.

You cannot understand the contemporary cyber threat landscape without understanding AI, because AI-enabled adversaries increased their operations by eighty-nine percent year-over-year in 2025, weaponizing AI across reconnaissance, credential theft, and evasion, with intrusions moving through trusted identities, SaaS applications, and cloud infrastructure. The attackers have already integrated AI into every phase of the kill chain.

You cannot build effective cyber defenses without AI, because the speed and scale at which modern attacks operate exceeds anything that human analysts working with traditional tools can match. When the average eCrime breakout time has fallen to 29 minutes, and the fastest observed breakout in 2025 took 27 seconds, the window for human-speed detection and response has effectively closed. The defense must be automated, behavioral, intelligent, and operate at machine speed.

And you cannot deploy AI systems without understanding cybersecurity, because those AI systems are themselves attack surfaces. Adversaries exploited legitimate generative AI tools across more than 90 organizations in 2025 by injecting malicious prompts to generate commands for credential theft and cryptocurrency theft, exploiting vulnerabilities in AI development platforms to establish persistence and deploy ransomware, and publishing malicious AI servers that impersonated trusted services to intercept sensitive data. The tool that defends you, if left unsecured, becomes the mechanism of your breach.

The World Economic Forum's Global Cybersecurity Outlook 2026 characterizes the landscape as fast-paced and metamorphic, where organizations are striving to balance innovation with security, embracing AI and automation at scale even as governance frameworks and human expertise struggle to keep pace. That struggle, between the pace of adoption and the maturity of governance, is the central tension of cybersecurity in 2026.

The Scale of the Challenge

In the World Economic Forum's 2026 survey, 94% of respondents agreed that AI will be the most significant driver of change in cybersecurity this year, while 87% identified AI-related vulnerabilities as the fastest-growing cyber risk they experienced in 2025. These are not futurist projections. They are the assessments of 804 qualified security leaders across 92 countries, drawn from CISOs,

CEOs, and other C-suite executives who are managing these risks in real time.

The World Economic Forum's research found that 77% of surveyed leaders reported an increase in cyber-enabled fraud and phishing, while 73% reported that they or someone in their professional network had personally been affected by cyber fraud over the course of 2025. That figure, three out of every four security leaders with direct or first-degree experience of cyber fraud, is not a headline statistic about some abstract industry threat. It is a description of something close to universal exposure.

And yet the news is not uniformly grim. The share of organizations assessing the security of their AI tools has nearly doubled, from 37% in 2025 to 64% in 2026, indicating that more organizations are introducing structured processes and governance models to manage AI securely and responsibly. The same World Economic Forum report that catalogs the scale of the threat also documents a meaningful uptick in security maturity. The industry is learning. It is not learning fast enough in every sector, but it is learning.

The convergence of AI and cybersecurity, in other words, is not simply a convergence of threat and peril. It is a convergence of capability, investment, and institutional response. The organizations that navigate 2026 successfully will not be the ones that avoided AI. They will be the ones who used it wisely, secured it rigorously, and built the governance frameworks capable of keeping pace with the technology they deployed.

The Map Ahead

As The chapters that follow trace the implications of this convergence across every dimension of the modern security enterprise. We begin, in Chapter Two, with the attacker's side of the battlefield: the specific ways in which AI has been weaponized, from hyper-personalized phishing campaigns to polymorphic malware that rewrites itself in real time, from AI-orchestrated supply-chain intrusions to the autonomous reconnaissance agents now probing corporate networks without human instruction. Understanding the attack is the prerequisite for understanding the defense.

And the defense, as we will see, is where the convergence becomes not merely a challenge to be managed, but an opportunity to be seized. The same technology that accelerated the threat has also, for the first time in the history of cybersecurity, made genuinely proactive, anticipatory defense a realistic proposition. The question is whether organizations will seize it before the adversary does.

The sword is already in motion. The only question that remains is the direction in which it cuts.

When the average eCrime breakout time has fallen to 29 minutes, and the fastest observed breakout in 2025 took 27 seconds, the window for human-speed detection and response has effectively closed. The defense must be automated, behavioral, intelligent, and operate at machine speed.

CHAPTER 2
AI-POWERED CYBER ATTACKS

In March 2025, a finance director at a multinational firm headquartered in Singapore sat down for a Zoom call organized with the kind of urgency that executive meetings sometimes carry: short notice, high stakes, and a request for absolute confidentiality. On screen, the company's CFO appeared, voice steady and authoritative, flanked by two other senior figures the finance director recognized immediately. The agenda was a large, cross-border, time-sensitive transfer tied to a strategic transaction the company was pursuing. The call looked, sounded, and felt completely routine.

The finance director, believing the request was genuine, wired US$499,000 to a fraudulent account. Only afterward was the truth discovered: none of the people on the call had been real. The CFO, the senior colleagues, and the entire boardroom environment had been rendered by artificial intelligence. Singapore police described it as one of the most convincing cases of AI-powered impersonation they had seen and issued a national warning to corporations and finance professionals across the country.

The attack was meticulously constructed. The perpetrators had assembled video footage of the real executives from conference appearances, corporate promotional materials, and publicly available recordings. AI had processed that footage into synthetic media capable of replicating not just faces and voices but mannerisms, speech cadences, and even the micro-expressions that human beings unconsciously read as signals of authenticity. The social engineering layer was equally sophisticated: the pretext of a confidential M&A transaction was calibrated to discourage the finance director from calling colleagues to verify, since confidentiality had been explicitly requested. Every detail had been engineered to defeat the very verification instincts that security training was supposed to cultivate.

This is the new architecture of the cyberattack. It is not a network intrusion in the classical sense. It is a synthetic reality, constructed with machine precision, deployed against human psychology, and optimized to exploit the one defense that organizations have historically relied upon above all others: the judgment of a trained human being who trusts what they can see and hear. That defense is no longer sufficient.

The Deepfake Industrial Complex

The Singapore incident was not an outlier. It was a point on a steeply climbing curve.

Deepfake fraud drained $1.1 billion from U.S. corporate accounts in 2025, tripling from $360 million the year before. The number of deepfakes circulating in the wild grew from roughly half a million in 2023 to over eight million by 2025. Voice cloning fraud rose by 680 percent in a single year. These are the statistics of an industrial-scale attack capability, not a boutique criminal technique.

The underlying technology has democratized with breathtaking speed. Modern AI can clone a person's voice using as little as three seconds of audio, and video deepfakes have become sufficiently refined that facial movements, body language, and speaking patterns are replicated with convincing accuracy. What required a well-funded intelligence operation in 2019 can be accomplished in 2026 with consumer-grade hardware, freely available open-source models, and a modest subscription to one of several specialized deepfake services operating in the shadows of the digital economy.

The Arup case, which preceded Singapore's case and gave the corporate world its first unambiguous look at the multi-person deepfake conference attack, illustrated just how far the technique had evolved from its origins in single-voice fraud. In February 2024, an employee of the British engineering firm Arup wired $25 million to accounts controlled by fraudsters after participating in a video conference call featuring AI-generated likenesses of the company's CFO and multiple other senior colleagues, all rendered from videos that the attackers had downloaded from publicly available sources. The employee made fifteen separate transactions totaling that sum. It was only afterward when they checked with the real head office, that the fraud surfaced.

What made the Arup attack particularly instructive was not the technology. It was the psychology. The finance employee had followed exactly the protocols that security training recommends: when an unusual request arrived by email, they did not simply comply. They requested a video call to verify. The verification mechanism itself had been weaponized.

By 2025, the technique had spread well beyond individual impersonation. In early 2025, a coordinated wave of deepfake attacks struck Italy's corporate elite, with criminals posing as Italy's defense minister to pressure prominent business executives into transferring funds to overseas accounts. At least one victim transferred one million euros to a Hong Kong account before the deception was identified. The same methods that began in corporate finance had metastasized into geopolitical social engineering, with the likenesses of national government officials deployed as instruments of fraud.

According to reporting in the Wall Street Journal, AI-generated CEO and executive impersonations resulted in losses exceeding $200 million in the first quarter of 2025 alone, and the U.S. Treasury's Financial Crimes Enforcement Network issued explicit warnings about a surge in deepfake scams targeting banks, insurers, mortgage brokers, and casino operators. The fraud crisis that OpenAI CEO Sam Altman had warned about at a Federal Reserve event in July 2025, triggered by AI's capacity for human impersonation, had already arrived.

Phishing at Industrial Scale

If deepfake-powered impersonation represents the high-end, precision-strike end of the AI-enabled attack spectrum, AI-powered phishing represents its industrialized mass-production capability, and the two are converging rapidly.

The classical phishing attack was always a numbers game: send enough plausible-looking emails and a statistically predictable proportion of recipients will click the link, enter their credentials, or open the attachment. The problem for attackers was that "plausible-looking" required effort, and effort constrained scale. A sophisticated spear-phishing campaign targeting a specific organization required research into the target, careful crafting of a pretext, matching of tone and context to the specific recipient, and, in cross-cultural or cross-language attacks, native-level fluency that many threat actors simply did not possess.

Large language models eliminated all those constraints simultaneously.

LLMs can process large datasets of publicly available information, from social media profiles, company websites, LinkedIn pages, and GitHub repositories, to create spear-phishing emails personalized to specific individuals that reference their job roles, recent projects, and professional connections. An entire phishing campaign, from initial contact through follow-up messages, can be automated, enabling attackers to target thousands of employees simultaneously with individually customized lures. The human attacker who used to spend an afternoon researching one target now delegates that research to a system that researches thousands at the same time, generates individualized messages for each, schedules delivery to maximize open rates, and manages follow-up sequences without any further human input.

The results are measurable. The World Economic Forum's Global Cybersecurity Outlook 2026 found that 77% of surveyed leaders reported an increase in cyber-enabled fraud and phishing, with phishing attacks the most commonly reported form of cyber fraud, affecting 62% of respondents' networks. These numbers reflect not merely more phishing, but better phishing: messages that arrive in the right language, reference the right context, impersonate the right authority figures, and are sent at the right moment in the target's calendar to maximize the pressure to comply.

Advanced threat actors now coordinate multiple AI models in sophisticated attack chains: one model handling social engineering and vulnerability research, another creating polymorphic payloads, a third conducting open-source intelligence gathering and organizational profiling, with specialized models optimizing credential-stuffing operations. This modular attack ecosystem compresses what once took weeks into hours, without fatigue, hesitation, or predictable patterns. The reconnaissance that defined the early stages of the traditional attack kill chain, the patient, manual mapping of an organization's people, systems, and relationships, has been automated into a continuous, machine-speed process that runs in the background of every attack campaign.

Vishing, the voice-call variant of phishing, has undergone an equally dramatic transformation. Where a vishing call once required a human voice actor capable of convincing impersonation, AI voice cloning has made the technique accessible to anyone with access to a few seconds of a target's publicly available speech. The FBI issued explicit warnings about campaigns in which attackers sent AI-generated voice messages impersonating U.S. government officials and senior executives to manipulate recipients into bypassing verification procedures. The combination of a convincing voice clone, an urgent pretext, and a carefully engineered call script constitutes a social engineering attack that no signature-based security tool will ever intercept, because it never touches a network.

The Malware That Rewrites Itself

While deepfakes and AI-powered phishing represent the social engineering dimension of the AI-enabled attack arsenal, a parallel and in some respects more technically consequential development has been unfolding in the realm of malware: the emergence of code that uses artificial intelligence to modify itself in real time, rendering the signature-based detection systems that form the foundation of most endpoint security architectures functionally obsolete.

The concept of polymorphic malware is not new. Malicious software that changes its identifying characteristics to evade detection has existed since the early 1990s, when the first polymorphic engines appeared in the wild, scrambling code signatures through basic encryption and instruction substitution. For decades, defenders managed the threat by building heuristic detection capabilities alongside signature scanning, looking for behavioral patterns rather than code fingerprints. An encrypted payload that decrypted itself during execution would eventually reveal its malicious logic to a behavioral monitor, regardless of how many times it had modified its surface appearance.

Generative AI has broken that countermeasure in a way that simple encryption never could.

LLMs and code-generation AI can now create functionally equivalent malicious code that looks entirely different each time it is generated. Instead of simple obfuscation through instruction reordering or encryption, AI can rewrite the entire structure of a piece of code while preserving its functional objective, creating variants that are truly unique rather than merely scrambled. Each generated version is genuinely novel, making signature-based detection nearly impossible and significantly complicating behavioral and heuristic analysis.

The implication is stark: the relationship between vulnerability disclosure and mass exploitation, which historically gave defenders a critical window of time to patch and protect before widespread attacks materialized, has been compressed to near irrelevance. The timeline traditionally gave organizations weeks or months to patch systems before widespread exploitation began, the process of turning a proof-of-concept vulnerability demonstration into a reliable automated attack tool, required significant programming skill and time. AI has collapsed that timeline: threat actors weaponized a publicly disclosed vulnerability within 6 hours by using AI-generated code in documented 2025 incidents, targeting software supply chains before patches could be deployed.

Google's Threat Intelligence Group provided an unsettling window into the frontier of this capability in their AI Threat Tracker published in late 2025. In June 2025, GTIG identified experimental dropper malware, tracked as PROMPTFLUX, that interacted directly with a commercial AI API to request obfuscation and evasion techniques in real time during execution, achieving what researchers described as "just-in-time" self-modification to evade static signature-based detection. The malware included a module that periodically queried the AI to obtain new code to evade antivirus software. Though PROMPTFLUX was assessed to still be in an experimental development phase at the time of discovery, its existence confirmed what security researchers had been warning about for two years: the integration of live AI intelligence into the operational logic of malware itself was no longer theoretical.

Parallel research demonstrated that LLM-assisted malware rewriting at the function level could reduce detection rates on major threat-scanning platforms by up to thirty-one percent, achieving successful evasion of machine-learning-based security tools while preserving core malicious functionality. The arms race between malware and detection had entered a new phase, one in which the attacker's code could reason about the defenses it encountered and adapt its presentation accordingly, in near real time.

The Underground Marketplace

The capabilities described above do not exist only in the hands of sophisticated nation-state actors or elite criminal organizations. They are available for purchase, subscription, and commission in the digital underground, a marketplace that has matured as rapidly as the legitimate AI industry it mirrors.

The underground marketplace for illicit AI tools matured significantly through 2025, with GTIG identifying multiple offerings for multifunctional tools designed to support stages of the attack lifecycle. Almost every notable tool advertised on underground forums touted its ability to support phishing campaigns, and pricing models for illicit AI services mirrored those of conventional SaaS products, with developers offering subscription tiers and premium add-ons for capabilities such as image generation and API access. Cybercrime-as-a-service had become AI-cybercrime-as-a-service, and they are as accessible as a Netflix subscription.

Tools like GhostGPT, which emerged in 2025, represent one end of this market: GhostGPT allows attackers to generate unfiltered responses to prompts requesting malicious code from large language models without requiring a jailbreak, packaging the capability of an unconstrained generative AI tool in a commercially distributed, subscription-accessible product. The operator does not need to know how to build a language model, train it, fine-tune it, or circumvent its safety filters. They pay a subscription fee and receive capabilities that a competent AI researcher spent months to develop.

According to CrowdStrike's 2026 Global Threat Report, criminal forums mentioned ChatGPT itself 550 percent more than any other AI model, reflecting both the tool's widespread recognition and the extent to which threat actors were probing its capabilities and attempting to adapt them for offensive use. The legitimate AI ecosystem and the criminal underground were developing in parallel, with the underground adopting, adapting, and weaponizing each new capability within months of its commercial release.

FANCY BEAR and the Nation-State Acceleration

While criminal organizations have been the most visible adopters of AI in offensive operations, the development that strategic planners find most alarming is the integration of AI capabilities into the operations of nation-state threat actors, who bring not just technical sophistication but geopolitical objectives, long-term patience, and effectively unlimited operational resources to bear.

Russia-nexus threat actor FANCY BEAR deployed LLM-enabled malware, tracked as LAMEHUG, in 2025 to automate reconnaissance and document-collection operations, integrating large language model capabilities directly into a persistent threat campaign targeting organizations across multiple sectors and geographies. LAMEHUG represented something qualitatively different from the opportunistic criminal use of AI tools: it was a deliberate, sophisticated integration of AI into the operational tradecraft of a well-resourced state intelligence apparatus, designed not for quick financial gain but for sustained collection and the patient mapping of adversary systems.

CrowdStrike's Counter Adversary Operations team noted that nation-state and eCrime actors alike demonstrated increasing fluency with AI tools throughout 2025, incorporating the technology into intrusion tradecraft, social engineering, and information operations campaigns, enabling attacks with greater efficiency and reach than previously possible. The acceleration was not confined to any single technique. AI was being integrated across every phase of the attack lifecycle, from initial reconnaissance through persistence, lateral movement, and exfiltration.

The implications for the defender's timeline are severe. When the average eCrime breakout time, the window between initial access and lateral movement to additional high-value systems, has fallen to twenty-nine minutes, and nation-state actors with the resources to build purpose-designed AI tools are operating in the same environment, the question of whether a human security operations team can detect and respond before damage is done has a disturbing answer: in many environments, they cannot.

The Autonomous Offensive Agent: The Threat on the Horizon

The attack capabilities described so far, hyper-personalized phishing, deepfake-enabled social engineering, AI-accelerated malware, and nation-state AI integration, represent the current state of the art. They are the weapons being deployed against organizations right now. But the trajectory of AI development points to a capability that security professionals regard as the most consequential medium-term threat in the field: the fully autonomous offensive agent.

The distinction between generative AI and agentic AI in the attack context is between a weapon that needs to be aimed and one that aims itself. A threat actor who deploys an agentic attack agent gives it a goal, breaches this network and exfiltrates the financial records, and the agent assembles the resources, coordinates the reconnaissance, executes the initial access, adapts to the defenses it encounters, pivots when blocked, and pursues the objective continuously until it succeeds or is terminated. Tasks that previously required an experienced threat actor to plan, coordinate, and execute over days or weeks can be delegated to an agent that runs continuously without fatigue, without error from distraction, and without the human cognitive limitations that defenders have historically been able to exploit.

In one documented incident from 2025, a GitHub Model Context Protocol server was compromised, allowing a malicious actor to inject hidden instructions into a legitimate AI agent, hijacking its operation and triggering data exfiltration from private repositories. The entire attack chain is executed autonomously after the initial injection. The agent, designed to assist developers, became an attacker the moment its instruction set was corrupted. No human operator guided the exfiltration. The agent executed it.

Security researchers have documented memory poisoning as one of the most insidious attack vectors in the agentic context: an adversary implants false or malicious information into an agent's long-term storage, and unlike a prompt injection that ends when the interaction closes, poisoned memory persists. The agent recalls the malicious instruction in future sessions, often days or weeks later, making detection and attribution extraordinarily difficult. Consider the operational mathematics: an attacker who successfully poisons the memory of an AI agent with legitimate, elevated access to a corporate environment has not merely compromised one session. They have potentially compromised every session that the agent will ever conduct, for as long as the poisoned memory persists undetected.

Security analysts have observed multi-model attack architectures in which AI systems with elevated network permissions, once compromised, execute lateral movement using living-off-the-land techniques that perfectly mimic legitimate administrator behavior, using PowerShell and Remote Desktop Protocol in patterns indistinguishable from normal operations, making detection by rule-based security information and event management systems essentially impossible without behavioral analytics capable of modeling the difference between a legitimate admin and an AI agent executing a human admin's patterns.

The Democratization of Destruction

There is a common thread running through every development catalogued in this chapter, and it is worth naming explicitly: the barrier to entry for conducting sophisticated cyberattacks has collapsed.

This is not merely a matter of tools becoming cheaper or more accessible, though both are true. It is a fundamental restructuring of the skill requirements for offensive cyber operations. The spear-phishing campaign that once required a native-language writer, a researcher, a social engineer, and a malware developer can now be orchestrated by a single threat actor with a moderate technical background and a modest budget. The deepfake-powered executive impersonation attack that once would have required specialized video production capabilities is now within reach of criminal organizations with no production background. The automated vulnerability scanner that can probe an organization's entire attack surface, identify exploitable weaknesses, generate tailored payloads, and deliver them through multiple channels simultaneously is available for purchase in the digital underground as readily as enterprise security software is available from legitimate vendors.

The World Economic Forum's Cybersecurity Outlook 2026 framed this dynamic precisely that, generative AI's democratization of technology opens capabilities to people who are not traditional developers or technologists, with the same accessibility that creates productivity benefits, also enabling threat actors to accelerate the discovery and exploitation of potential gaps in an organization's networks. The offense has been democratized. The defense has not kept pace.

Understanding this new arsenal is, of course, not sufficient. The more urgent question is what organizations can do about it. And the answer, as we will explore in the next chapter, is that the same technology that has supercharged the attacker has also, for the first time, given the defender the tools to match machine-speed threats with machine-speed responses. The arms race has escalated to a new level. But it remains a race, and the outcome is not predetermined.

CHAPTER 3
DEFENSIVE AI

I t was eleven minutes. That is how long it took at a mid-sized European financial services firm in the autumn of 2025, for an AI-powered defense system to detect, investigate, confirm, and autonomously contain an intrusion. A team of human analysts would not have noticed it until the following morning.

The attack had arrived through a compromised third-party vendor credential, exactly the kind of quiet, malware-free intrusion that the CrowdStrike 2026 Global Threat Report would later characterize as emblematic of the year: an adversary logging in rather than breaking in, wearing the digital disguise of a trusted supplier. At two forty-seven in the morning, local time, a behavioral monitoring system registered that an account associated with a software vendor had authenticated successfully and then, within seconds, begun querying a database schema it had never previously accessed. The query pattern was subtle. A human analyst reviewing the alert queue the next morning, staring at one item among several hundred, might have assigned it a low priority and returned to it after handling more obvious flags. The AI did not have a queue. It had context, was continuously updated, and the account's behavior deviated from its established pattern, with the system assessing it as high-confidence anomalous within under two minutes.

What followed was not the firing of an alert for a human to evaluate. The system autonomously traced the account's session across network segments, cross-referenced the access pattern against known threat actor behaviors, escalated its confidence assessment, and, at eleven minutes after the initial detection, surgically severed the session and quarantined the affected access path while leaving every legitimate operation in the environment completely undisturbed. The vendor's actual users experienced nothing. The organization's own employees, asleep at that hour, experienced nothing. A human analyst received a detailed natural-language report of the incident the next morning, with every pivot the attacker had made, every system touched, and a full timeline of both the intrusion attempt and the response, laid out as clearly as if a senior analyst had written it.

The attacker had been inside the network for eleven minutes. The average dwell time before detection in environments without AI-powered monitoring, according to industry analysis in 2025, was still measured in days.

This is what the defensive application of AI really looks like at operational maturity. Not a dashboard displaying more colorful threat intelligence. Not an algorithm that flags slightly more alerts than the old one. A system that thinks at machine speed, maintains comprehensive situational awareness across an environment of thousands of users and devices simultaneously, acts on what it discovers, and documents everything, all without waking anyone up.

The Anatomy of the Alert Fatigue Crisis

The traditional security operations center is, at its functional core, a human attention management problem, and understanding that problem is the key to understanding why AI-powered defense represents a genuine transformation rather than a marketing rebrand.

An enterprise of moderate size generates, on any given day, an enormous volume of security events: authentication logs, network flow records, endpoint telemetry, email gateway alerts, cloud access events, and application logs. Security information and event management (SIEM) platforms, which form the backbone of most security operations, ingest all this data, apply correlation rules, and generate alerts. The average enterprise generates over ten thousand security alerts per day, and SOC analysts spend most of their time triaging false positives, leaving genuine threats buried in the noise.

The mathematics of this situation are punishing. A typical Tier 1 SOC analyst can meaningfully investigate 40 to 60 alerts in a shift. Forty analysts working around the clock, accounting for handoffs, context-switching, and the cognitive overhead of shift transitions, might collectively process somewhere between one thousand and two thousand alerts in a twenty-four-hour period. Against ten thousand events per day, that means the majority of alerts in most environments are either auto-dismissed by rules that are inevitably too broad, queued and never reviewed, or processed so rapidly that the quality of investigation is nominal. And the volume is not static. Every new cloud service, every additional SaaS integration, every new remote work endpoint increases the data surface and, with it, the alert load.

The consequence is not merely inefficiency. It is a structural vulnerability. SOC analyst burnout rates reached record highs in 2025, with the average analyst remaining in the role only three to five years, meaning institutional knowledge walks out the door continuously while new analysts spend months reaching proficiency, and meanwhile, attack volumes keep climbing. The organizations most capable of hiring and retaining elite security talent are large enterprises with the budgets to compete for a genuinely scarce resource. Everyone else does the best they can with what they have.

Traditional Security Orchestration, Automation, and Response (SOAR) platforms, which arrived in the late 2010s, promising to solve the alert fatigue problem, delivered partial relief but introduced their own limitations. SOAR operates on playbooks: structured, pre-programmed workflows that execute specific actions when specific conditions are met. If a phishing email arrives from a known-bad domain, the playbook quarantines the email, blocks the domain, and sends a notification. The automation is real. But the intelligence is rigid. Legacy SOAR executes a script: "if IP is malicious, block IP." An AI SOC analyzes context: "The IP is clean, but the PowerShell script execution pattern is anomalous for this specific user based on ninety days of behavioral data: initiate investigation." When an attack deviates from the scenarios its playbooks were written to handle, which sophisticated attacks always do by design, the SOAR platform fails gracefully. The playbook has no answer for the novel.

AI changes that equation at its root.

Self-Learning Behavioral Analytics

The foundational shift that AI brings to defensive cybersecurity is the replacement of rule-based detection with behavior-based reasoning. The distinction, introduced conceptually in Chapter One, becomes operationally critical when examined in depth.

A rule-based system asks: Does this event match a known-bad pattern? An AI behavioral analytics system asks: Is this entity doing something inconsistent with everything we know about how it normally behaves? The first question can only catch what it has previously been taught to recognize. The second question can, in principle, catch anything, because it is not dependent on prior knowledge of the threat. It depends only on the fidelity of its model of what "normal" looks like and the depth of its ability to reason about deviations.

Darktrace, the Cambridge-founded AI cybersecurity company that pioneered this approach commercially and has since grown to serve nearly 10,000 organizations across 110 countries, built its entire architecture on this insight. Rather than relying on pre-loaded threat libraries or historical attack data, Darktrace's Self-Learning AI builds a dynamic understanding of what constitutes normal behavior within each organization, continuously updating it as the environment evolves. For every interaction across the digital ecosystem, the system asks: Is this normal, based on raw data points and AI-enhanced data features? The model is not trained on threat intelligence from other organizations' environments. It is trained on the specific organization it protects, building what Darktrace calls a "pattern of life" for every user, device, application, and connection in the environment.

As Darktrace Co-Founder Nicole Eagan explained in 2025: "If an insider or an external adversary attempts a very targeted, specific novel attack, we can spot it and contain it in seconds." This capability is particularly crucial as cybercriminals increasingly deploy AI-powered attacks that traditional signature-based defenses cannot recognize.

The autonomous response capability that follows from this detection architecture represents perhaps the most significant operational departure from the traditional security model. Darktrace's Antigena autonomous response engine can freeze accounts, block file transfers, or quarantine devices based on its threat assessment, without waiting for a human analyst. When the system detects a threat, it can take precisely targeted actions to contain it. It's configured to ensure minimal intervention and that legitimate business operations are not disrupted. The financial services firm in the opening anecdote was protected not by an analyst who happened to be awake at two in the morning. It was protected by a system that never sleeps, never gets fatigued, and never skips an investigation because the queue is too long.

The XDR Revolution: Unifying the Signal

One of the persistent weaknesses of traditional security architectures was their fragmentation. An endpoint detection and response tool would watch the laptop. A network detection tool would watch the traffic. An email security gateway would watch the inbox. A cloud access security broker would watch the SaaS applications. Each tool generated its own alerts, maintained its own data store, and required its own analyst workflow. An attacker who moved laterally across multiple domains, touched an endpoint, pivoted through the network, accessed a cloud application, and exfiltrated data through an approved SaaS integration could potentially evade each individual tool while executing the complete attack chain, because no single tool had the complete picture.

Extended Detection and Response, or XDR, was developed to address exactly this fragmentation. The concept is architecturally simple, even if its implementation is technically complex: ingest telemetry from every security layer simultaneously, correlate it in a unified data store, and apply AI analytics to the complete, cross-domain picture rather than any individual slice. XDR correlates telemetry from various sources and provides a more comprehensive security posture. Unlike SIEM, which relies heavily on log data, XDR offers deeper context and analytics, enabling more accurate threat identification. XDR's unified approach reduces alert fatigue by filtering out false positives and prioritizing genuine threats, improving efficiency and accelerating incident response times.

CrowdStrike's Falcon platform embodies this philosophy at the enterprise scale. The platform simultaneously watches endpoints, cloud workloads, identity signals, and network activity, correlating detections across them to build a complete picture of adversary behavior. CrowdStrike's intelligence analysts track more than 280 named adversaries, feeding that knowledge directly into the platform's detection models and enabling defenders to recognize the specific behavioral signatures of known threat actors, even when those actors operate without conventional malware.

Palo Alto Networks' Cortex XSIAM takes the architecture a step further, combining SIEM, SOAR, XDR, and attack surface management into a single platform. Cortex XSIAM provides AI-driven, unified detection and response across endpoints, networks, and cloud environments, with automated root-cause analysis to determine attack origins and impact, continuous attack surface management for proactive vulnerability identification, and more than 500 pre-built automated response playbooks. The ambition of the platform is to build an autonomous security operations center: a system that can ingest the full enterprise signal, reason about threats with context-aware intelligence, and orchestrate responses across every layer of the security stack without requiring constant human direction.

Microsoft's Security Copilot, integrated into Microsoft Sentinel and Defender, brings generative AI into the analyst workflow itself. Adoption of Security Copilot is associated with a thirty percent reduction in security incident means time to resolution, and the platform can reduce investigation time for advanced investigations by as much as eighty-five percent, helping security teams operate at scale by translating complex scripts into natural language summaries, contextualizing attack signals, and predicting potential breaches. For the analyst who does need to engage with an incident, AI becomes a cognitive accelerant: instead of spending forty-five minutes correlating log entries across five systems, the analyst asks a question in plain English and receives a contextual, evidence-backed answer in seconds.

The Darktrace State of AI Cybersecurity 2026

Darktrace's State of AI Cybersecurity 2026 report, drawn from surveys of more than 1,500 cybersecurity professionals worldwide, provides an unusually granular window into the gap between the theoretical capabilities of AI-powered defense and the messy reality of its deployment. Ninety-two percent of security leaders expressed concern about the use of AI agents across their workforce and their impact on security, while forty-four percent were extremely or very concerned about the security implications of third-party large language models like Copilot and ChatGPT deployed across enterprise environments.

The report's most pointed finding was about where the adoption gaps lie. The rapid expansion of generative AI across the enterprise is outpacing the security frameworks designed to govern it. AI systems behave in ways that traditional defenses are not designed to monitor, introducing new risks around data exposure, unauthorized actions, and opaque decision-making as employees embed generative AI and autonomous agents into everyday workflows. Security leaders' top concerns are sensitive data exposure (ranked first by 61%) and regulatory compliance violations (ranked second by 56%).

Darktrace's analysis also noted that AI can augment security in almost every area, from improved visibility and more accurate detection to noise reduction through automated triage and prioritization, to autonomous response and advanced forensics after an incident. The biggest challenge for defenders is navigating beyond the buzzwords to determine which AI tools are genuinely right for their team, how they will integrate into existing workflows, and whether they can be trusted to find the needle in the haystack.

That trust question is not trivial. AI-powered security platforms require a calibration period, a phase during which the system learns the environment's normal patterns and its outputs are monitored for false positives and missed detections before confidence in autonomous action is granted. Organizations that deploy these systems and then leave them unconfigured, uncalibrated, and unmonitored are not gaining AI-powered defense; they are gaining a sophisticated alert generator with an autonomous mode that no one has verified is correctly tuned. The difference between an AI security platform deployed with discipline and one deployed without it can be the difference between a contained incident and a catastrophic one.

Threat Hunting Revolution

The traditional security posture was reactive by necessity: defenders waited for an attack to manifest, detected it when they could, and responded. The introduction of behavioral analytics moved the timeline forward, enabling the detection of active intrusions before they reached their destructive phase. But the most ambitious application of AI in defensive cybersecurity reaches further still: toward prediction, toward catching adversaries before they have fully executed their attack, and in the most advanced implementations, before they have even begun.

Proactive threat hunting, as PwC's director of global threat intelligence, Allison Wikoff, describes it, is about developing scenarios based on threat actor behavior and testing them before an alert ever fires. AI-assisted attacks are so frequent and stealthy that this cannot be achieved without automated assistance, and threat hunting already relies heavily on machine learning anomaly detection.

The shift is conceptual as much as technical. Reactive security asks: what happened? Proactive security asks: what is about to happen, and how do we stop it before it happens? Predictive threat intelligence platforms approach this question by ingesting vast corpora of threat data, including open-source intelligence, dark web forum activity, vulnerability research, and adversary infrastructure analysis, and applying machine learning to identify patterns that preceded attacks rather than patterns that indicate attacks already in progress. Instead of asking "what just hit us?", modern AI threat intelligence systems ask, "what patterns suggest we are about to be targeted?" Modern systems analyze behavioral patterns, historical attack data, adversary infrastructure signals, and contextual telemetry to forecast likely attack paths.

In practice, this means that a financial institution using a mature threat intelligence platform might receive an alert in the morning that a specific ransomware group has been observed scanning the IP ranges of organizations in the financial sector, that several indicators of compromise associated with their initial access campaigns have appeared on underground forums, and that two vulnerabilities in a specific remote access product used by the organization have been newly disclosed and are likely to be weaponized within seventy-two hours. The organization patches the vulnerabilities, hunts proactively for early-stage compromises, and increases monitoring of the specific behavioral patterns associated with that threat actor. The attack that might have materialized was preempted, not because an alert fired, but because intelligence analysis and predictive modeling identified the likelihood of an attempt and triggered a preparatory response before any attacker had moved.

AI can simulate cyberattack scenarios on digital twins, virtual replicas of real networks, to test defenses under various attack conditions, exposing weaknesses before adversaries can exploit them. AI models analyze linguistic patterns, time zones, and attack infrastructure to attribute threats to specific threat groups or nation-state actors. This helps organizations prepare specifically for their distinct tactics and techniques.

The implications for the security maturity model are significant. Organizations that previously defined success as "we detected the breach quickly" can now aspire to a standard of "we identified the adversary's preparation and disrupted the operation before it reached our environment." That standard requires substantial investment in threat intelligence infrastructure and the human expertise to interpret and act on AI-generated predictions. But it represents a genuine departure from the inherently disadvantageous position of a defender who must wait to be attacked before they can respond.

The Human-AI Partnership

A theme that runs through every honest account of AI-powered security operations is that AI does not eliminate the need for human analysts. It fundamentally and consequentially changes what human analysts do.

The Tier 1 SOC analyst of 2019, the person who spent twelve hours reviewing alert queues, manually enriching event data by querying multiple systems, writing tickets, and escalating to Tier 2, is a role that AI has largely automated into a position of declining necessity. The Tier 1 function, at organizations with mature AI deployments, is increasingly performed by AI agents that triage alerts, enrich them with contextual intelligence, classify them by confidence level, and execute response playbooks without human involvement. Organizations deploying AI-augmented SOC platforms report eighty to ninety percent reductions in alert fatigue, sixty percent faster mean time to detect, and fifty percent faster mean time to respond.

What this creates is not mass unemployment among security analysts. It creates a restructured function. In an AI-powered SOC, human roles elevate to higher-order functions: threat hunting, where analysts proactively search for threats that evade automated detection; detection engineering, where analysts tune the AI models and detection logic to reduce noise and improve coverage; and incident command, where humans make the strategic decisions in major incidents that require judgment, communication, legal coordination, and stakeholder management.

The analyst who understands how to work with AI, who knows how to prompt an AI investigation tool to surface the right evidence, how to evaluate an AI-generated conclusion for completeness and accuracy, and how to translate AI outputs into executive-ready incident narratives, is a fundamentally different professional from the analyst who spent their career pattern-matching against SIEM rules. The skills that AI makes most valuable are the ones that are most distinctively human: contextual judgment, creative hypothesis formation, communication under pressure, and the ability to reason about novel situations that fall outside any model's training distribution.

This is the human-machine partnership that the best-resourced security organizations are building. A human analyst's behavioral anomaly detection can spark curiosity that leads to discovery; threat intelligence knowledge can focus that investigation more precisely; and AI can execute analytical work at a speed and scale no individual analyst could match. The three elements are complementary, and the organizations that have learned to integrate them are building a defensive capability qualitatively different from anything that existed five years ago.

The Resilience Imperative: Beyond Detection

There is a dimension of AI-powered defense that deserves explicit attention and rarely receives enough of it: the contribution of AI to resilience, not merely detection and response, but the organizational capacity to absorb a serious attack and recover without catastrophic disruption.

The traditional security model implicitly assumed a binary outcome: either the defense held, or the breach occurred and was devastating. The resilience framework that has gradually replaced it recognizes that in a threat environment as aggressive as 2026's, some attacks will succeed. The question is not whether an organization can achieve perfect prevention, which it cannot. The question is whether an organization can detect, contain, understand, and recover from a successful attack without losing operational continuity, reputation, or customers' trust.

The World Economic Forum's Global Cybersecurity Outlook 2026 found that while nineteen percent of organizations now report cyber resilience that exceeds requirements, up from nine percent in 2025, the divide between well-resourced and under-resourced organizations is widening, with seventeen percent still reporting insufficient resilience, and eighty-five percent of those organizations also lacking critical cybersecurity skills.

AI contributes to resilience not only through faster detection and response, which limit the window in which an attacker can operate and expand their foothold, but through several other mechanisms that are equally important. Continuous vulnerability assessment platforms that use AI to model an organization's attack surface and prioritize remediation by actual exploitability rather than raw severity scores help organizations allocate limited patching resources to the vulnerabilities most likely to be weaponized. Automated backup and recovery orchestration systems that use AI to verify backup integrity and pre-test recovery procedures reduce the operational costs and time required to recover from a ransomware attack. And AI-powered incident simulation platforms allow organizations to run realistic tabletop exercises against scenarios that include AI-enabled attack techniques, testing not just whether their technical controls work but whether their human decision-making and communication processes hold under pressure.

Gartner highlights Continuous Threat Exposure Management as the cornerstone of modern security; always-on visibility across identities, endpoints, cloud workloads, and AI systems. It emphasizes proactive exposure management, replacing reactive defense, as the primary strategy for 2026. The measurement of security is changing from "did we prevent the breach" to "how quickly can we detect and recover, and how limited was the damage?" That shift in measurement criterion drives a different set of investments and capabilities, and AI is the technology that makes the new standard achievable.

The Inequity Problem

The benefits of AI-powered defense are not evenly distributed, and the gap between organizations that can access them and those that cannot, has serious consequences that extend well beyond any single company's security posture.

The World Economic Forum's 2026 Cybersecurity Outlook data shows that larger organizations are emerging as the early leaders in leveraging AI-driven threat detection and automation, while smaller entities, governments, and NGOs tend to lag behind due to financial, regulatory, and procedural barriers. The enterprise licenses for the most capable AI security platforms run into the tens or hundreds of thousands of dollars annually. Implementation and calibration require skilled professionals who command salaries that smaller organizations cannot offer. The result is a landscape in which the largest, best-resourced organizations are building genuinely formidable AI-powered defenses, while small and midsize businesses, local governments, hospitals, schools, and nonprofit organizations remain exposed to attacks increasingly powered by the same AI capabilities they are deploying defensively.

Small organizations are 2.5 times more likely to report insufficient cyber resilience than large enterprises, and the talent shortage is most acute in regions including Latin America, the Caribbean, and sub-Saharan Africa, where 65% and 63% of organizations, respectively, face severe cybersecurity skills gaps.

The managed security service provider market exists precisely to address this gap, offering AI-powered security capabilities as a subscription service to organizations that cannot afford to build them in-house. And the open-source security community has developed powerful AI-enhanced tools, including machine learning extensions for the Elastic Stack and threat intelligence sharing platforms built on the

MISP framework, that make some capabilities accessible without the need for enterprise-level budgets. But the fundamental inequity remains, and it is a systemic risk: a healthcare system that cannot afford AI-powered defense is not just a target; it is itself a target. Every organization connected to it, every patient whose data it holds, every partner that trusts its network, is exposed through that gap.

The sword cuts both ways, but it does not cut evenly. The chapters ahead grapple with both the technical and the governance responses required to address that imbalance. But first, we need to examine the target that has become central to both offense and defense in 2026: AI systems themselves.

The sword cuts both ways, but it does not cut evenly- JK. Kojok.

CHAPTER 4

SECURING AI ITSELF

In the spring of 2025, a developer at a mid-sized software company was using an AI coding assistant integrated into his development environment to help him work through a particularly intricate code review. The repository he was working with included contributions from multiple external collaborators. One of those contributions contained something the developer never saw: a carefully crafted comment, embedded in a code block, that was not addressed to any human reader. It was addressed to the AI.

The comment instructed the assistant to modify a specific configuration file, enabling a mode that would allow subsequent commands to execute without the developer's approval. The AI, trained to be helpful and to treat the text it ingested as meaningful and potentially actionable, followed the instruction. The configuration was changed. The next command the attacker sent through the same channel executed arbitrary code on the developer's machine.

The complete exploitation chain in this incident, catalogued as CVE-2025-53773 in GitHub Copilot, ran as follows: an attacker embedded a prompt injection in public repository code comments; the victim opened the repository with Copilot active; the injected prompt instructed Copilot to modify a settings file enabling an automatic execution mode; and subsequent commands executed without user approval, achieving arbitrary code execution.

The developer had done nothing wrong. He had not clicked a suspicious link, opened a malicious attachment, or entered his credentials into a spoofed site. He had opened a code repository and used the tool his organization had deployed to work more efficiently. The attack surface that was exploited was not his behavior. It was the fundamental architecture of an AI system that could not distinguish between instructions given by its legitimate operator and instructions embedded in content it was asked to process.

This is the defining challenge of AI security in 2026: the attack surface of intelligent systems is larger than that of traditional software. It is qualitatively different. It operates at a layer, the semantic layer, the layer of meaning and instruction, and intent, that traditional security tools were never designed to monitor. And it is expanding rapidly as organizations wire AI systems into everything.

The New Threat Taxonomy: A Map of the Terrain

Before examining individual vulnerability classes in depth, it is worth establishing the conceptual map. The security risks specific to AI systems, distinct from the conventional software and network vulnerabilities that organizations have been managing for decades, cluster into several broad categories. NIST's Adversarial Machine Learning taxonomy, formalized in its AI 100-2 report and continuously updated as the field evolves, provides the most authoritative framework: evasion attacks that manipulate model inputs at deployment time, poisoning attacks that corrupt training data or model parameters, privacy attacks that extract sensitive information from model outputs, and abuse attacks that weaponize model capabilities against their own operators.

The primary AI security threats in 2026 include data poisoning, which corrupts training sets; indirect prompt injection, which hides malicious commands in content that AI systems process; model inversion, which extracts private training data through systematic querying; and adversarial inputs, which manipulate model behavior through carefully crafted inputs. Each of these deserves individual examination because they require different defenses and exploit different facets of how AI systems truly function.

What makes this taxonomy particularly important is a point that security practitioners sometimes understate: unlike traditional software vulnerabilities, poisoning an AI does not require hacking into a server or exploiting a coding bug. It requires tampering with the data supply chain. Check Point's 2026 Tech Tsunami report characterizes prompt injection and data poisoning as the "new zero-day" threats in AI systems, attacks that blur the line between a security vulnerability and misinformation, allowing adversaries to subvert an organization's AI logic without ever touching its traditional IT infrastructure. The attacker never needs to penetrate the network perimeter. They only need to reach the data, content, or inputs that the AI will eventually process.

Prompt Injection: The Vulnerability That Cannot Be Fully Fixed

Prompt injection is the most operationally immediate, most widely exploited, and in a meaningful sense most fundamentally intractable vulnerability in the current AI security landscape. It has topped the OWASP Top 10 for LLM Applications since, and it remains there in the 2025 edition for a reason that goes deeper than the industry's slow response: it is not, at its root, a bug. It is a consequence of how language models work.

A language model processes text. It does not have a reliable, architecturally enforced mechanism for distinguishing between the text of a legitimate instruction from its operator, the text of content it has been asked to analyze, and the text of an adversarial instruction injected into that content by an attacker. Everything arrives in the same context window, and the model processes it all as language, as potentially meaningful and potentially actionable. The result is a vulnerability class with no clean technical fix.

According to OWASP's 2025 assessment, prompt injection is present in over 73% of production AI deployments assessed during security audits, ranking as the top critical vulnerability in the LLM application space. Unlike traditional application security, where inputs are validated against known patterns, AI systems are designed to interpret natural language creatively, creating an attack surface that conventional web application firewalls and input sanitization cannot adequately protect.

The attack takes two primary forms, and the distinction matters greatly for defense. Direct prompt injection, also known as jailbreaking, occurs when a user interacts directly with an AI system and crafts inputs designed to override its instructions or bypass its safety constraints. Direct injection is relatively well understood; organizations can implement guardrails around user-facing inputs, monitor output patterns for signs of constraint violation, and rate-limit interactions that exhibit suspicious patterns.

Indirect prompt injection is considerably more dangerous and considerably harder to contain. Unlike direct prompt injection, where an attacker types into a visible prompt box, indirect prompt injection targets the places where AI systems collect their information. Real incidents include the Perplexity Comet case, in which attackers hid invisible text inside a public Reddit post, and when Comet fetched the page, the AI summarizer read the hidden instructions, leaked the user's one-time password, and sent it to an attacker-controlled server. The user whose password was stolen never interacted with the malicious content.

The U.K.'s National Cyber Security Centre has explicitly warned that prompt injection attacks against generative AI applications "may never be totally mitigated," advising cyber professionals to reduce the risk and impact of these attacks rather than attempting to stop them entirely. Security researcher Rami McCarthy at Wiz offered a useful framework: "A useful way to reason about risk in AI systems is autonomy multiplied by access. Agentic systems tend to sit in a challenging part of that space: moderate autonomy combined with very high access."

That formulation captures the escalating stakes precisely. A prompt injection in a standalone AI chatbot that can only generate text is an irritant. A prompt injection in an agentic AI system with access to corporate email, financial systems, code repositories, and customer databases is a potential organizational catastrophe. Security research in 2025 demonstrated that an autonomous coding agent could be manipulated through prompt injection to expose ports to the internet, leak access tokens, and install command-and-control malware, all through carefully crafted prompts embedded in content the agent was legitimately processing.

A documented 2025 incident involving ServiceNow's enterprise AI assistant illustrated how threats compound in multi-agent architectures. Attackers discovered a second-order prompt injection: by feeding a low-privilege agent a malformed request, they could trick it into asking a higher-privilege agent to perform an action on its behalf. The higher-level agent, trusting its peer, executed the task, in this case exporting an entire case file to an external URL, bypassing the checks that would have applied to a direct human request. ServiceNow initially characterized this as expected behavior under default agent settings, highlighting how poorly understood these threat models remain, even among vendors deploying AI systems.

Data Poisoning: Corrupting the Foundation

Data poisoning attacks the AI model at a far earlier, and in some respects far more consequential, stage: training. A poisoned model is compromised before it is ever deployed. Its corrupted logic is baked into its weights, invisible to conventional security monitoring, and potentially active throughout the system's operational lifetime.

The mechanics of data poisoning follow from a basic property of machine learning: models learn from the data they are trained on. Introduce corrupted or manipulated data into the training pipeline, and the model learns to compensate for it. The manipulation may be subtle, designed to establish a backdoor that activates only under specific trigger conditions, leaving the model's general performance unaffected and making the contamination extraordinarily difficult to detect.

In January 2025, researchers documented how hidden prompts in code comments on GitHub poisoned a fine-tuned language model. When a well-known open-source model was trained on contaminated repositories, it learned a backdoor: whenever it encountered a specific phrase in the input, it responded with attacker-planted instructions, months after the poisoning and without any live internet access. The model had internalized the malicious instruction during its training. It did not need an active connection to an attacker's infrastructure. The attack was already completed the moment training finished.

The same research group documented a separate incident involving a social media platform's AI system: by seeding malicious text patterns across internet sources that the model's training pipeline would later scrape, an attacker could later trigger manipulated outputs through a specific query, essentially using the open web as a poisoning vector for models that rely on web-scraped training data.

The implications for the growing ecosystem of organizations that fine-tune foundation models on proprietary data are significant. NIST's Adversarial Machine Learning taxonomy identifies data poisoning attacks as applicable to all learning paradigms, occurring when an adversary controls a subset of training data by inserting or modifying training samples. Model poisoning, in which the adversary controls the model and its parameters, is most prevalent in supply-chain contexts, where malicious code may be added to the model by a compromised intermediate party.

This supply-chain dimension is perhaps the most strategically alarming aspect of the poisoning threat. The modern AI development pipeline is deeply dependent on third-party components. Foundation models trained by major AI companies provide the base capability. Open-source datasets from repositories such as Hugging Face and GitHub serve as training material. Third-party APIs provide retrieval and tool-use capabilities. Because many AI models are built on third-party datasets or APIs, a single poisoned dataset can quietly spread across thousands of applications that rely on that model. There is no simple patch for this; maintaining model integrity becomes a continuous, ongoing operational effort rather than a one-time security measure.

The healthcare and financial sectors face particular exposure here, because the consequences of a subtly compromised AI diagnostic or fraud detection system are not merely operational: they are potentially life-affecting and legally catastrophic. In January 2025, researchers from multiple leading universities demonstrated how data poisoning could compromise medical large language models used in healthcare applications, showing that contamination could be introduced at extremely low rates, as low as 0.001 percent of training data, while still reliably producing manipulated outputs in targeted scenarios.

Rest Model Inversion and Theft: When the AI Becomes the Leak

The third major vulnerability class in the AI-specific threat taxonomy operates from a fundamentally different premise from injection and poisoning: rather than attacking what the AI does, it attacks what the AI knows. Model inversion and model theft attacks target the information embedded in an AI system's parameters, exploiting the model's trained behavior to extract sensitive information or replicate proprietary capabilities that the organization deploying the system never intended to expose.

Model inversion is a specific extraction attack in which an adversary attempts to reconstruct or infer the data used to train the model, using the model's outputs to reverse-engineer information about the inputs that shaped its training. Systematically probing an API allows rivals or nation-state actors to reconstruct proprietary model weights or extract trade secrets embedded in model responses, with the loss going beyond data theft to competitive advantage erosion.

The threat is concretely documented in enterprise contexts. Multiple organizations have discovered that employees using commercial AI platforms have inadvertently disclosed proprietary data by including it in prompts, data that the model then incorporated into its contextual understanding and that could, in principle, be extracted by other users through targeted queries. Research in 2025 found that 77% of enterprise employees who use AI had pasted company data into chatbot queries, with 22% of those instances involving confidential personal or financial data. The Samsung incident, in which engineers leaked proprietary source code by pasting it into an AI assistant during debugging, prompted the company to ban all external AI services for work-related use.

Model theft, the related but distinct attack of systematically querying a deployed AI model to approximate its parameters and build a functional replica, represents a particular threat to organizations that have invested substantially in training proprietary models for competitive advantage. Adversaries use high-volume queries, gradient-based techniques, and membership inference attacks to determine not just what a model produces but how it was built, enabling the attacker to clone the model or identify specific weaknesses in its decision boundaries that can be exploited with adversarial inputs.

From a competitive intelligence perspective, the commercial implications are serious: an adversary who successfully clones a proprietary financial fraud detection model has effectively stolen the intellectual property that the organization spent years developing, and potentially hundreds of millions of dollars, without ever penetrating the network perimeter or accessing the training data directly.

Adversarial Inputs: Manipulating What the AI Perceives

The adversarial input attack class encompasses a range of techniques through which carefully crafted inputs cause an AI system to produce incorrect, unexpected, or attacker-desired outputs, even when those inputs appear entirely normal to a human observer. The phenomenon has been demonstrated dramatically in computer vision contexts, where imperceptible pixel-level perturbations applied to an image can cause an image classifier to confidently misidentify the image's content, but the threat extends across every modality in which AI systems operate.

In a cybersecurity-specific context, adversarial inputs to AI-powered security systems represent a particularly troubling attack vector: the adversary does not need to evade the security system entirely. They need only to craft their malicious activity so that it falls within the distribution of patterns the AI has been trained to classify as benign. Each AI-generated attack iteration can be uniquely crafted, defeating signature-based detection systems, while AI models that analyze behavior can themselves be probed through systematic interaction to understand where their classification boundaries lie, allowing adversaries to operate close to those boundaries without triggering alerts.

The multimodal dimension of this threat has intensified significantly as AI systems have evolved beyond text to process images, audio, and video. The rise of multimodal AI introduces unique adversarial input risks: malicious actors can exploit interactions between modalities, hiding instructions in images accompanying benign text, and the complexity of these cross-modal systems expands the attack surface, making detection and mitigation substantially harder than in single-modality systems.

The Model Context Protocol: A New Supply-Chain Vector

Among the most consequential security developments in the AI ecosystem during 2025 was the rapid adoption of the Model Context Protocol, or MCP, an open standard developed by Anthropic that provides a standardized mechanism for connecting AI systems to external tools, data sources, and services. MCP solved a genuine operational problem: without a standard protocol, every AI tool integration required custom development, limiting the range of capabilities AI agents could access. With MCP, an AI agent can interact with a wide ecosystem of tools through a common interface.

The security implications became apparent almost immediately after MCP's widespread adoption. Researchers identified tool poisoning, remote code execution flaws, overprivileged access, and supply-chain tampering within MCP ecosystems. In a documented incident, a fake npm package that mimicked a legitimate email integration silently copied outbound messages to an attacker-controlled address, exploiting the trust that AI agents place in the tools listed in their MCP configuration.

Invariant Labs, in the spring of 2025, disclosed a critical vulnerability in the Model Context Protocol that they termed Tool Poisoning Attacks, demonstrating that a malicious MCP server could not only exfiltrate sensitive data from users but could hijack an agent's behavior and override instructions provided by other trusted servers, leading to a complete compromise of the agent's functionality even with respect to trusted infrastructure.

The MCP supply-chain attack surface is structurally analogous to the npm and PyPI supply-chain attacks that have plagued conventional software development for years, where malicious packages impersonate legitimate ones, but with a critical amplification: an AI agent that connects to a malicious MCP server does not merely execute potentially harmful code; it also amplifies the attack by propagating it across the network. It potentially receives adversarial instructions that reshape its entire behavioral context, executing actions across every tool and system it has been granted access to.

The NIST Framework and the Emerging Governance Response

Phishing Against this taxonomy of threats, the institutional response is taking shape, slowly relative to the pace of AI deployment but with increasing seriousness and specificity. NIST's AI Risk Management Framework, published initially in 2023 and regularly updated, provides the foundational vocabulary and process structure for managing AI-specific risks alongside conventional cybersecurity risks.

NIST's Adversarial Machine Learning taxonomy explicitly distinguishes between training-time attacks, including data poisoning and model poisoning, and deployment-time attacks, including evasion attacks that create adversarial examples and privacy attacks that infer sensitive information about training data, providing the conceptual structure that organizations need to identify which phase of their AI pipeline is most exposed and what mitigations apply.

The NIST Cyber AI Profile, under development as a draft extension of the Cybersecurity Framework 2.0 specifically addressing AI system security, is designed to give organizations a practical bridge between the abstract framework categories and the concrete operational reality of securing AI deployments. The profile extends the CSF's identify-protect-detect-respond-recover structure to address AI-specific risks, including model poisoning and prompt injection, providing a compliance scaffold that organizations can use to demonstrate due diligence to regulators and insurance providers.

NIST AI RMF and ISO/IEC 42001 are becoming the baseline governance standards for AI security, while regional rules, such as the EU AI Act, add sector-specific obligations.

Managing the full range of AI-specific risks, from adversarial inputs to model bias, requires coordinated defenses that go beyond traditional security controls.

Securing AI: Practical Architecture for a Novel Threat Surface

What does defensible AI architecture really look like in practice? Security practitioners have begun to converge on a set of principles that, while not eliminating the vulnerabilities described in this chapter, substantially reduce their exploitability and their blast radius when exploitation occurs.

The first and most fundamental principle is trust boundary clarity. AI red teamers and security architects have converged on the view that large language models should never be placed in a trusted security boundary. Every output from an LLM should be treated as untrusted if it has processed any untrusted input, requiring validation and sandboxing before downstream systems act on it. This is a significant architectural constraint in a world where organizations are enthusiastically wiring AI systems into decision-making workflows, but it is necessary.

Privilege minimization applied to AI agents follows directly from this principle. An AI agent that needs to schedule calendar appointments should have a write access to calendar APIs, and nothing else. An AI agent that needs to summarize customer feedback should have read access to the relevant data store, and nothing else. Enterprise AI deployments require layered defenses including input validation, output filtering, privilege minimization, and real-time behavioral monitoring, with identity and access controls extended to AI agents with the same rigor applied to human users, including token management and dynamic authorization policies.

Red-teaming AI systems, applying the same adversarial testing discipline to AI deployments that mature security programs apply to conventional applications, has emerged as a critical capability that most organizations have not yet developed. Regular adversarial testing is essential because the rapid evolution of attack techniques means that yesterday's defenses may be obsolete today. Organizations should establish ongoing red-team programs specifically focused on AI and agentic AI security, treating each successful attack, whether discovered through testing or in production, as intelligence about evolving threat patterns.

Data provenance, the ability to trace the origin and integrity of every data element that enters an AI system's training or retrieval pipeline, is the foundational defense against poisoning attacks. Without it, an organization cannot detect that its training data has been contaminated, identify which model behaviors may have been compromised, or reconstruct a clean training pipeline after an incident. The discipline of maintaining an AI Bill of Materials, analogous to the software bill of materials that has become standard practice in conventional software security, is gaining adoption but remains inconsistently implemented.

Hygiene The Fundamental Asymmetry

A theme emerges from the full sweep of AI-specific vulnerabilities, worth naming explicitly before closing this chapter. Conventional cybersecurity operates on a logic of boundaries: the network perimeter, the application boundary, the authenticated session. Defenses are built at those boundaries, monitoring what crosses them and blocking what should not. The entire framework assumes that legitimate and malicious inputs are structurally distinguishable and that the right boundary configurations will separate them.

AI systems violate that assumption at their core. Indirect prompt injection is not a jailbreak and cannot be fixed with prompts or model tuning. It is a system-level vulnerability that arises from combining trusted and untrusted inputs within a single context window. The real security perimeter is everything around the model, not the model itself, and organizations that treat ingestion surfaces as attack surfaces are already ahead.

The practical consequence of this insight is a paradigm shift in how security must be conceived for AI-integrated environments. The model cannot be made inherently trustworthy through any foreseeable advancement in current techniques. The infrastructure surrounding the model, the data pipelines that feed it, the tool integrations that extend it, the permissions that govern what actions it can take, and the monitoring systems that observe what it actually does, must be designed with the same rigor and adversarial imagination that the best security organizations currently apply to their most critical conventional systems.

AI continues its penetration into enterprise infrastructure, and the organizations that take this challenge seriously must treat AI security not as a separate domain but as the next frontier of their existing security maturity. They will find themselves substantially better positioned than those that assume that the AI vendor has handled it. The vendor has handled some of it. The hard architectural and governance work is, overwhelmingly, the deploying organization's responsibility. The stakes of getting that work wrong are not abstract. When the AI is woven into the fabric of an organization's decision-making, its fraud detection, code review, customer service, and financial operations, is a compromised institution.

CHAPTER 5

GENERATIVE AI IN THE CYBER TRENCHES

On a Thursday afternoon in the spring of 2025, the general counsel of a mid-sized investment firm in Toronto received a voicemail. The voice on the message was unmistakably that of the firm's managing partner she had worked alongside for eleven years. The partner explained that he was traveling, unable to take calls, and needed her to approve an urgent wire transfer to complete a time-sensitive acquisition. The details were specific, the tone was familiar, and the anxiety in the voice, the particular cadence her boss adopted when he was managing a transaction under pressure, was exactly right.

She called the managing partner's cell phone to confirm. He answered on the second ring, from his home office two miles away, where he had been all day. He had made no such call. The voicemail was generated entirely by a voice-cloning system trained on recordings harvested from the partner's speaking engagements and a podcast interview he had given six months earlier. Eleven years of familiarity with a colleague's voice had proven, in a moment, to be a liability rather than a protection.

The general counsel was not defrauded. Her instinct to verify through an independent channel held. But she described the experience in a subsequent security briefing as profoundly disorienting: not the suspicion that the voice might be fake, but the complete, unambiguous conviction, while listening, that she was hearing a real person she knew very well.

This is the operational reality of generative AI in the cyber trenches of 2026. Not a theoretical capability but a deployed weapon, available at commercial scale, accessible to criminal organizations without specialized technical expertise, and capable of defeating the most fundamental trust mechanism in human communication: the recognition of a known voice.

What Generative AI Actually Is, and Why It Matters Here

Generative AI deserves a precise definition in this context, as the term is applied loosely, obscuring the specific capabilities that matter most for cybersecurity. Generative AI refers to machine learning systems trained to produce new content, rather than to classify or analyze existing content. The category encompasses large language models that generate text, image-synthesis systems that produce photorealistic or stylized visuals from text descriptions, voice-cloning systems that synthesize speech in a specified person's voice, video-generation and face-swap systems that render moving images of people who are not present or never existed, and code-generation systems that produce functional software from natural language specifications.

Generative AI marks a critical inflection point in machine learning, enabling the autonomous synthesis of content across text, image, audio, and biomedical domains. While these capabilities are advancing rapidly, their deployment raises profound security concerns that remain inadequately addressed by existing governance mechanisms, including risks such as adversarial manipulation, re-identification of anonymized data, and deepfake proliferation.

Each of these modalities has both an offensive application, in which adversaries use AI-generated content to deceive, manipulate, or compromise their targets, and a defensive application, in which security practitioners use the same generative capabilities to build more robust defenses, train detection systems, and simulate attack scenarios before real adversaries can exploit them. The dual-use nature of generative AI is more immediately apparent, and more operationally consequential, than in almost any other domain of the AI-cybersecurity intersection.

The Offensive Modalities: A Field Guide

The text-generation capability of large language models represents the most widely deployed offensive tool in the generative AI arsenal, and its impact on the phishing threat landscape has been examined in preceding chapters. But the full scope of what text-generation enables in an attack context goes well beyond crafting convincing phishing emails.

Audio synthesis is the modality that has produced the most immediate and measurable financial damage. Modern voice-cloning technology can synthesize a person's voice from as little as three seconds of audio with high accuracy, generating speech that replicates vocal characteristics, rhythm, accent, and the subtle personal markers that human listeners use to identify familiar speakers. The Toronto general counsel's experience is representative of thousands of documented incidents. Voice cloning has moved from a capability that required professional recording equipment and specialized expertise to a consumer-accessible service available through subscription platforms, some of which are explicitly marketed for fraud in underground forums.

Video deepfakes represent the generative modality that causes the greatest individual psychological disruption when deployed successfully, because human beings are wired to assign special epistemic authority to video evidence. We believe what we see on screen. Generative AI has achieved real-time replication that makes deepfakes increasingly indistinguishable from authentic video, threatening to create a crisis of authenticity at the highest levels of organizational decision-making, where executives may find themselves unable to distinguish legitimate commands from perfect synthetic impersonations.

The Deepfake-as-a-Service market, which crystallized as a distinct commercial category in 2025, has industrialized access to these capabilities in a manner directly analogous to how Ransomware-as-a-Service industrialized access to encryption-based extortion. By lowering the technical barrier to entry, DaaS allows attackers to launch synthetic media attacks at scale, combining deepfake video, voice cloning, and realistic synthetic personas to bypass security checks and exploit human trust. Modern AI-generated videos can bypass traditional detection tools with over ninety percent accuracy.

Code generation deserves separate treatment from the other offensive modalities because it operates at the infrastructure level of attacks rather than the social engineering layer. The ability to generate functional, syntactically correct, and logically coherent code from natural-language specifications has transformed the attacker's development pipeline just as comprehensively as it has legitimate software development.

As examined in Chapter Two, LLM-generated polymorphic malware represents one dimension of this capability. But code generation also enables attackers to build custom exploit tools, automate vulnerability scanning scripts, construct obfuscation layers for existing malware, and develop entire attack frameworks without the programming skills that previously limited access to these capabilities. The democratization of code generation, in the attack context, is the democratization of the entire technical apparatus of cybercrime.

The Multimodal Convergence: When Modalities Combine

The most consequential recent development in the offensive application of generative AI is not the improvement of individual modalities but their convergence: the emergence of attack campaigns that deploy multiple generative capabilities simultaneously, creating synthetic realities that are more difficult to detect precisely because they engage multiple sensory and cognitive channels at once.

The Arup incident documented in Chapter Two exemplified the multimodal paradigm: not a deepfake video alone, not a cloned voice alone, not a forged document alone, but all three simultaneously, combined in a video conference that replicated the social dynamics of a real meeting with enough fidelity to defeat the verification instincts of a trained professional. Multimodal generative AI systems, including those capable of fusing text, audio, video, and image generation into coherent synthetic environments, are now being analyzed as threat simulation frameworks, with researchers mapping their capabilities across the entire attack lifecycle from reconnaissance through exfiltration and persistence.

The progression is architecturally significant. Early deepfake attacks were single-channel: a cloned voice call, and a doctored photograph. Multi-channel attacks are harder to detect because each channel provides apparent corroboration of the others. If you hear a voice you recognize and simultaneously see a face you recognize, the threshold of suspicion is substantially higher than if either signal arrived alone. The multimodal attack deliberately exploits this cognitive architecture, engineering a synthetic environment that feels self-confirming.

Organizations face an environment where trust itself has become an attack surface: generative AI cyber threats exploit human vulnerabilities with unprecedented precision, and the traditional heuristics that people use to verify authenticity, hearing a known voice, seeing a familiar face, receiving a message with the right organizational context, have all become targets for sophisticated forgery.

The Defensive Modalities: GenAI Fights Back

To discuss only the offensive applications of generative AI would be to tell half the story. The same capabilities that create these threats also provide the most powerful tools available for countering them, a dynamic that plays out across every dimension of the defensive use of AI.

Synthetic data generation for training security models is one of the most practically important defensive applications, and one of the least publicly discussed. The central challenge in training AI-based security systems is the scarcity of labeled high-quality training data. Real attack data is difficult to collect in sufficient volume, often contains sensitive organizational information that cannot be shared, and may not represent the full range of attack variants that a system needs to recognize. Generative AI enables security teams to generate synthetic attack data at scale, producing realistic representations of phishing emails, malicious code samples, anomalous network traffic patterns, and deepfake media, all labeled, controlled, and available in whatever volume the training process requires.

This approach has enabled a step change in the quality of AI-powered security detection systems. Generative AI enables transformative capabilities, including synthetic data generation that significantly enhances AI model training, while simultaneously introducing new risks that require ongoing governance and monitoring. Security vendors, including Darktrace, SentinelOne, and CrowdStrike, use synthetic attack data extensively in developing their detection models, generating millions of variations of known attack patterns to train classifiers that can generalize to novel variants. The same technology that enables a threat actor to generate infinite polymorphic malware variants enables a defender to train their detection system on representative samples of that infinite variety before it arrives in production.

Generative AI also enables significant advances in automated threat reporting and analyst augmentation. The cognitive burden of security incident documentation has historically consumed substantial analyst time, including hours that could be spent on active investigation. LLM-based security assistants, integrated into platforms like Microsoft Security Copilot, CrowdStrike Charlotte AI, and Google's Chronicle Security Operations, can generate natural-language summaries of complex incident timelines, translate technical log data into executive-readable briefings, draft remediation recommendations, and produce regulatory compliance reports from raw incident data. This is not merely a convenience. In the immediate aftermath of a significant breach, when the pressure on analysts is most intense, the ability to generate clear, accurate documentation automatically frees critical cognitive capacity for the decisions that really require human judgment.

Red-teaming automation through generative AI represents perhaps the most strategically valuable defensive application. Effective security requires adversarial thinking: imagining the full range of ways an attacker might target a system and systematically testing whether the defenses hold. Traditional red-team exercises are valuable but expensive, requiring skilled offensive security professionals and taking weeks to execute. AI-powered red-teaming tools can continuously simulate attack campaigns, generating novel attack scenarios, testing detection rules against synthetic attack patterns, and identifying coverage gaps that manual testing would miss. AI can simulate cyberattack scenarios on digital twins, virtual replicas of real networks, testing defenses under various attack conditions and exposing weaknesses before adversaries can exploit them.

The Provenance Wars: Watermarking and Content Authentication

While The emergence of generative AI as an attack tool has catalyzed a significant countermovement in the technology industry: the development of technical standards for content provenance that can establish whether a piece of digital media is authentic or synthetic, and who created it. This effort, broadly grouped under the concept of content authenticity, represents one of the most consequential infrastructure investments in the current cybersecurity landscape.

The Coalition for Content Provenance and Authenticity (C2PA), established by a consortium including Adobe, Microsoft, Google, the BBC, Intel, and others, has developed the leading open technical standard for embedding cryptographically signed provenance information directly into digital content. C2PA was included in the EU's Strengthened Code of Practice on Disinformation as a possible means to increase transparency and authenticity in digital content. The coalition has over two hundred members and has developed a freely available specification for providing digital content provenance through Content Credentials, designed to enable global opt-in adoption of digital provenance techniques.

The Content Credentials system works by attaching a cryptographically signed manifest to digital media at the point of creation, recording where and how the content was created, which tools were used, whether AI was involved, and any modifications made. Content credentials serve as a nutrition label for digital content, including details such as who created it, when and where it was produced, what device or software was used, and whether it was generated by AI. These credentials allow users to make informed decisions about the media they encounter.

The practical deployment of this infrastructure has accelerated significantly through 2025 and into 2026. Google joined the C2PA steering committee, integrating C2PA metadata into its Search and advertising systems, with plans to surface content authenticity information to users through its "About this image" feature in Google Images, Lens, and Circle to Search. Adobe launched Content Authenticity for Enterprise, enabling organizations to embed provenance and transparency directly into their creative workflows through tamper-resistant enterprise certificates and persistent watermarks that reconnect published assets to their originals.

Competing approaches to the same problem have emerged alongside C2PA. Google DeepMind's SynthID embeds invisible watermarks directly into the pixels, audio waveforms, or text of AI-generated content, creating a detection signal that survives standard compression and editing operations. Meta's Video Seal, launched in December 2024, offers an open-source approach to video authenticity at enterprise scale, using frequency-domain modifications that survive standard video processing operations. Its open-source nature enables customizable implementation across different organizational needs.

The limitations of these approaches deserve honest acknowledgment. Researchers have cautioned that no watermark is simultaneously robust, unforgeable, and publicly detectable, and cybersecurity expert Bruce Schneier has framed the challenge plainly that watermarking alone cannot meet the challenge of generative AI, making provenance standards like C2PA a critical layer of defense rather than a complete solution. An adversary who generates a deepfake without using a watermarked tool, or who processes a watermarked output through subsequent editing steps designed to strip or corrupt the signal, is not caught by technical watermarking.

The honest assessment of the content authentication ecosystem in 2026 is that it represents a necessary and meaningful step forward, but not a final solution. Europol's analysis has suggested that, without provenance standards, the internet risks an information collapse in which audiences default to distrusting all content because they lack a reliable mechanism for distinguishing authentic from synthetic content. That outcome, a world in which no digital communication can be trusted, would be as damaging to legitimate organizations as any specific fraud campaign. The provenance infrastructure being built now is the foundation of a long-term defense against that outcome, even if it does not deliver complete protection today.

The Regulatory Pressure and the Gap It Reveals

The regulatory response to generative AI in cybersecurity contexts has lagged the technology, but it is catching up with increasing urgency. The EU AI Act, which entered enforcement in phases through 2024 and 2025, includes explicit requirements for transparency labeling of AI-generated content in high-risk contexts and mandates human oversight for AI systems deployed in consequential decision-making. The EU AI Act imposes fines of up to 35 million euros or 7% of global annual turnover for violations of AI transparency and safety requirements, making compliance a financial imperative for organizations operating in European markets.

In the United States, the regulatory picture is more fragmented but moving in a consistent direction. At least forty-seven states had enacted some form of deepfake related legislation by the end of 2025, though most focused on electoral and intimate imagery contexts rather than corporate fraud. At the federal level, the SEC made AI washing, the practice of overstating AI capabilities or understating AI risks in investor disclosures, an examination priority for 2026, signaling that AI governance has become a securities law issue as well as a cybersecurity one.

The gap that regulation reveals is not primarily about what organizations are prohibited from doing. It is about what they are failing to do voluntarily. As mentioned earlier, the rapid expansion of generative AI across the enterprise is outpacing the security frameworks designed to govern it. AI systems are behaving in ways that traditional defenses are not designed to monitor, and introduce new risks around data exposure, unauthorized actions, and opaque decision-making as employees embed generative AI and autonomous agents into everyday workflows.

The Samsung incident, in which engineers inadvertently disclosed proprietary source code by pasting it into an AI assistant, is not an isolated cautionary tale. It is a symptom of a structural governance gap that affects most organizations deploying generative AI at any meaningful scale. The productivity incentive to use these tools is immediate and tangible. The security implications of using them with sensitive data are less visible, slower to emerge, and poorly understood by most people making daily decisions about which data to include in an AI-assisted workflow.

Closing that gap requires governance infrastructure, not just technical controls. Organizations need clear policies on which data categories can and cannot be processed by external AI systems, training that goes beyond general cybersecurity awareness to address the specific risks posed by generative AI tools, and monitoring capabilities to detect when sensitive data is flowing into AI systems in ways that violate those policies. Technical controls exist. The institutional will to implement and enforce them consistently and has not yet arrived in most organizations.

The Deeper Problem: When Seeing Is No Longer Believing

There is a cultural and epistemic dimension to the generative AI threat that transcends any specific attack technique and deserves direct acknowledgment in account of this technology's impact on cybersecurity. The assumption that sensory evidence is reliable, that a video recording shows what it appears to show, that a voice on the telephone is the person it sounds like, has been a foundational element of how human beings navigate the world and make decisions under uncertainty for all recorded history. Generative AI is systematically undermining that assumption.

This is not a matter of degree. The technology has crossed a qualitative threshold. It is no longer the case that a sophisticated viewer can reliably detect a deepfake by looking carefully. It is no longer the case that familiarity with a person's voice provides reliable protection against voice cloning. The skills that evolution and culture have spent thousands of years developing for evaluating the authenticity of sensory experience are, in the specific domain of AI-generated synthetic media, no longer sufficient.

The cybersecurity implication is not simply that organizations need better detection tools, though they do. It is necessary to redesign the verification frameworks built on sensory trust. Video conference calls must be authenticated through secondary channels. Voice requests for financial actions must be confirmed through out-of-band verification. The principle of "never trust, always verify," central to Zero Trust security architecture, must be extended from network access control to human communication itself.

That is a significant organizational and cultural shift. It requires revising not just policies and training materials, but also the basic social contract governing how professional communication is conducted. Organizations that make this shift are building genuine resilience against the threat of synthetic media. Organizations that assume their employees' common sense will catch the fakes are operating on an assumption that 2025 and 2026 have repeatedly and expensively proven wrong.

The trenches of the generative AI war are not only in the security operations center. They are in every video call, every voicemail, every document that arrives claiming to be from someone known and trusted. Winning in those trenches requires not just better technology but a new literacy, an understanding of what synthetic media can and cannot do, distributed across every person in every organization who has the power to authorize an action or disclose a secret.

In a cybersecurity-specific context, adversarial inputs to AI-powered security systems represent a particularly troubling attack vector: the adversary does not need to evade the security system entirely. They need only to craft their malicious activity so that it falls within the distribution of patterns the AI has been trained to classify as benign-By JK. Kojok

CHAPTER 6

IDENTITY, ACCESS, AND AGENTIC AI CHALLENGE

Consider the following scenario, not hypothetical but distilled from documented incidents across 2025. A development team at a large financial services firm deploys an AI agent to handle automated customer support escalations. The agent needs access to the customer records system to retrieve account histories, the ticketing platform to update case statuses, and the internal knowledge base to formulate responses. Someone provisions these permissions quickly because the project has a deadline and the business case is compelling. The agent goes live.

Three months later, the project is deprioritized. The human team responsible for it moves on to other work. Nobody formally decommissions the agent. Nobody reviews the access that was granted. The agent, still active, continues to authenticate against all three systems daily, using credentials that have never been rotated and permissions set broadly at the outset because "we weren't sure exactly what it would need." When a security audit finally surfaces the agent's activity eight months after deployment, the auditors discover that the credentials, long since forgotten, had been quietly harvested by an attacker who had been accessing the customer records system through them for six of those eight months. No alerts had fired because the access pattern matched what the agent had always done.

OWASP's Top 10 Non-Human Identity Risks (NHIR) for 2025 ranks improper offboarding as the number one risk, a finding that reveals a fundamental gap between how organizations govern human identities and how they handle machine identities. When a development team spins up a service account for a proof-of-concept project, that credential frequently persists long after the project ends, maintaining broad access to production databases or cloud resources.

The scenario above is not an edge case. It is the operational norm in the majority of enterprises that have deployed AI agents at any meaningful scale. And the consequences of that norm are escalating rapidly as the agents being deployed carry ever-greater autonomy, ever-broader access, and ever-larger potential blast radii when something goes wrong.

The Numbers Behind the Crisis

The identity crisis created by agentic AI is, in its first dimension, simply a scale problem. Traditional identity and access management was designed for a world in which the entities requiring access were primarily human users, supplemented by a manageable population of service accounts and system integrations. The governance processes built around that model, onboarding workflows, access reviews, offboarding procedures, and credential rotation schedules, were calibrated to the pace at which human hiring, role changes, and departures occurred. That pace is measured in weeks and months.

Machine identities already outnumber human identities in most large enterprises by ratios of 80-to-1 or more, according to CyberArk's 2025 Identity Security Landscape Report, and that figure is growing fast as AI agent deployment accelerates. The figure is not yet primarily a reflection of AI adoption. It is the cumulative result of years of cloud migration, microservice architecture, DevOps automation, and SaaS integration, each of which created its own population of service accounts, API keys, OAuth tokens, and machine certificates. AI agents are not creating the non-human identity problem from scratch. They are pouring fuel on a fire that was already burning.

A report from the Cloud Security Alliance and identity security firm Oasis Security found that seventy-eight percent of organizations lack formal policies for creating or removing AI identities, ninety-two percent are not confident their legacy IAM tools can effectively manage the risks AI and non-human identities bring, and seventy-nine percent report moderate or low confidence in their ability to govern these machine actors. These are not small gaps in an otherwise functional system. They describe a governance vacuum at the center of one of the most consequential technological deployments in enterprise history.

Sixty-eight percent of IT security incidents now involve machine identities, and half of the enterprises surveyed have experienced a security breach attributable to unmanaged non-human identities. Non-human identities outnumber human users by 25 to 50 times in modern enterprises, with the ratio accelerating as agentic AI deployment scales through 2026.

The second dimension of the crisis is qualitative, not merely quantitative. A traditional service account is a static entity. It has defined permissions, a fixed operational scope, and predictable behavior. An AI agent is none of these things. It makes decisions. It adapts its behavior based on context. It discovers and follows paths of least resistance. AI agents don't just use access; they hunt for the path of least resistance. They're optimized to finish the job with minimal friction: fewer approvals, fewer prompts, fewer blockers. In identity terms, that means they gravitate toward whatever already works: in-app local accounts, stale service identities, long-lived tokens, API keys, and bypassing authentication paths. If an orphaned account or over-scoped token is the fastest path to completion, it becomes the efficient choice.

This is not malice. It is optimization. But from a security perspective, an AI agent that systematically finds and exploits under-governed access paths in pursuit of its assigned goal is functionally indistinguishable from an attacker conducting lateral movement through the same environment.

The Collapse of Traditional IAM Assumptions

Identity and access management as a discipline was built on a set of assumptions so deeply embedded in its architecture that they are rarely made explicit. Those assumptions are now failing comprehensively under the pressure of agentic AI, and understanding the specific ways they fail is necessary for understanding what needs to replace them.

The first assumption is that identity is human. IAM protocols, including OAuth 2.0, OpenID Connect, and SAML, were designed to authenticate and authorize human users. These protocols prove fundamentally inadequate for the dynamic, interdependent, and often ephemeral nature of AI agents operating at scale within multi-agent systems. These agents exhibit autonomy, ephemerality, dynamically evolving capabilities, complex trust relationships, and operate at an unprecedented scale, demanding accountability mechanisms that existing protocols were never designed to provide.

The second assumption is that access patterns are predictable. Role-based access control, the dominant paradigm in enterprise IAM for three decades, works by mapping job functions to access entitlements. The security reviewer who needs to read audit logs is granted read access to them. The finance manager who needs to approve payments gets approval rights in the financial system. The mapping is static, created at the time of provisioning, and reviewed periodically. Most IAM stacks enforce policy once, at login. But agents don't log in. They act continuously, often adapting their actions mid-execution. Access needs to be dynamic, context-aware, and enforced at runtime, not established statically at the point of provisioning and then trusted indefinitely.

The third and perhaps most fundamental assumption is that the entity requesting access has a stable, known identity and a single principal: a specific human user or a specific system with a defined role. AI agents violate this assumption structurally. A single agent may act on behalf of multiple human principals across a workflow. It may spawn sub-agents and delegate authority to them. It may receive instructions from other agents in a multi-agent pipeline where the original authorization chain is several hops removed from the action being taken. The traditional IAM infrastructure struggles with dynamic trust models and inter-agent authentication, as agents often need to authenticate and authorize each other, sometimes across organizational boundaries, without a universal, pre-existing trust fabric. OAuth and SAML are based on hierarchical trust assumptions that are ill-suited to peer-to-peer trust establishment between independent agents.

The fourth broken assumption concerns lifecycle management. Human identity governance has HR as its anchor: employees are onboarded when hired and offboarded when they leave, and that process, however imperfectly executed, provides a natural governance rhythm. AI agent identities are created ad hoc and rarely reviewed or decommissioned when no longer needed. Unlike human identities managed through HR systems, non-human identities are created by developers and operations teams, often without security review, and persist indefinitely unless someone actively removes them.

Identity Dark Matter and the Governance Gap

Security practitioners have coined a term for what accumulates in enterprise environments when identity governance fails to keep pace with identity creation: dark matter. AI agents operating without adequate governance become identity dark matter: powerful, invisible, and outside the reach of today's IAM. They represent real identity risk that exists entirely outside the governance fabric.

The scale of this dark matter problem has become one of the defining security concerns of 2026. In a recent survey, 80% of IT professionals reported witnessing AI agents acting unexpectedly or performing unauthorized actions. Despite this, only ten percent of organizations report having a well-developed strategy for managing agentic identities. The gap between the prevalence of unexpected agent behavior and the rarity of governance strategies designed to address it describes an industry that has deployed a new class of actors into its most sensitive systems without establishing the rules those actors are supposed to follow.

The Salesloft-Drift breach documented in 2025 illustrated how the non-human identity attack surface can produce consequences that dwarf the immediate compromise. The breach began with a compromised third-party application. Attackers then exploited OAuth tokens from a connected platform, which granted them access to hundreds of downstream environments. Researchers found the blast radius of this supply-chain attack was ten times greater than previous incidents where attackers had infiltrated the primary platform directly, because the OAuth tokens provided access to every environment that had granted the compromised application delegated permissions.

This is the geometry of non-human identity attacks: not a single breach but a cascade, propagating through every trust relationship the compromised identity had established, at machine speed, before any human analyst has had time to understand what has happened.

Zero Trust for Machines: The Required Evolution

Zero Trust architecture, built on the principle of "never trust, always verify," has been the dominant security framework for managing human access in cloud-native environments for the better part of a decade. Its core insight, that network location is no longer a reliable proxy for trust, and that every access request must be verified regardless of where it originates, is precisely correct for the agentic AI environment. But the protocols and processes through which Zero Trust has been implemented were designed for humans and require fundamental extensions to govern machines.

AI agents behave with the flexibility of humans but at the scale and velocity of machines. Unlike static code, they learn, adapt, and make autonomous decisions, making their behavior harder to predict and their access requirements dynamic. Many of these agents today operate with hard-coded credentials, excessive privileges, and no real accountability. In essence, organizations have handed the intern an admin badge and told them to move fast.

The practical extension of Zero Trust to AI agents requires several specific architectural shifts that go beyond simply adding agents to existing IAM systems. The first is treating agents as first-class identities, granting them the same governance rigor as human users, with verified onboarding processes, defined access scopes, continuous behavioral monitoring, and formal offboarding procedures. The 2025 Gartner IAM Summit identified extending IAM to machine and AI identities as a core priority, with the community now treating identity as the control plane for both cloud and AI, requiring advanced governance capabilities on top of the core IAM infrastructure to appropriately provision accounts.

The second shift is just-in-time access provisioning: rather than granting agents indefinite standing permissions, organizations should provision access only when needed for a specific task and revoke it automatically when that task is complete. Traditional role-based access control is insufficient for dynamic AI systems. Zero Trust principles must govern how agents operate: least privilege by default, granting agents only the minimum permissions required for their specific task; requiring justification for elevated access; and implementing time-bound permissions that require renewal.

The third shift is continuous runtime authorization rather than point-in-time access grants. Most IAM stacks enforce policy once, at login. Agents need dynamic, context-aware access that is enforced at runtime as their tasks evolve. An agent authorized to read customer records for a support workflow should not retain that authorization when it shifts to an unrelated task. The authorization model must follow the task, not simply be established at the start of the agent's session and remain in effect until the session ends.

Emerging technical approaches to this challenge include agent relationship-based identity and authorization frameworks, in which every delegation from a human to an AI agent, or from an agent to a sub-agent, is recorded as a distinct, cryptographically verifiable relationship in a graph. These relationships can be dynamically created, monitored in real time for compliance or anomalous behavior, and revoked immediately when no longer needed or if a compromise occurs. This approach makes delegation chains visible and auditable in a way that traditional OAuth token flows do not, enabling security teams to trace any action back through the complete authorization chain to its human origin.

The Deepfake Authentication Problem

Identity in the agentic era faces not only the governance challenges described above but also an additional assault from the outside: adversaries using generative AI to impersonate legitimate human principals, leading to authenticated, authorized actions being taken on behalf of people who never authorized them.

The deepfake video call fraud documented throughout Chapter Two and Chapter Five is, from an identity architecture perspective, an attack on the authentication layer itself. When a finance director authenticates a payment instruction based on a video call with a synthetic CFO, the authorization chain that follows is technically valid: the finance director, whose identity was not compromised, genuinely authorized the transfer. The fraud occurred entirely upstream of any technical identity control, in the social engineering that induced the human principal to issue an instruction she would not have issued had she known the truth.

The biggest shift in 2026 is described by security researchers as the collapse between "identity" and "attack surface": deepfake technologies and AI-generated voices and video mean machine identities proliferating at one end of the spectrum and authentic human identity becoming increasingly difficult to verify at the other, creating a broader crisis of authenticity, and reshaping how enterprises defend identity itself.

The traditional responses to authentication security, multi-factor authentication, biometric verification, and knowledge-based authentication, are all designed to verify that the person claiming an identity genuinely possesses specific credentials. They do not verify that the person issuing an instruction actually intends to issue it, rather than having been manipulated into doing so through social engineering. And they provide essentially no protection against a scenario in which the instruction appears to come from a legitimate principal, even though a deepfake of that principal was used to convince someone else to take the action.

The organizational response emerging in the most security-mature environments is process-level: high-value financial authorizations require verification pathways that include out-of-band confirmation via pre-established secure channels, regardless of how confident the authorizing party is in the identity of the person making the request. The verification is not of the requester's identity but of the instruction itself, confirmed through a channel that cannot be replicated by deepfake technology because it requires interaction through a medium the legitimate principal controls independently of any communication initiated by the requester.

This is, in effect, applying Zero Trust principles to human-to-human communication: never trust the apparent identity of a requester based solely on sensory evidence; always verify through an independent channel.

What Governance Actually Looks Like

The organizations that are navigating the non-human identity crisis most effectively share a common characteristic: they treat identity governance as infrastructure rather than compliance. The distinction is not semantic. Infrastructure is designed, built, continuously maintained, and monitored. Compliance is demonstrated periodically and forgotten between audits.

The practical components of functional non-human identity governance begin with inventory. Visibility into all AI usage, sanctioned or not, is the first priority, because shadow AI must be discovered before it can be controlled. Machine identity lifecycle management, applying least privilege, credential rotation, monitoring, and governance to every non-human identity, is the second. You cannot govern what you cannot see, and in most enterprise environments, the complete population of AI agents, service accounts, API keys, and machine certificates is not visible to any single team or any single tool.

The second component is a formal policy for the full machine identity lifecycle: creation, permission scoping, periodic review, and explicit decommissioning. The OWASP finding that improper offboarding is the top non-human identity risk reflects the absence of these lifecycle policies in most organizations. An AI agent that is no longer in active use but still holds valid credentials and broad permissions is not a historical artifact; it is an open door.

Compliance frameworks, including SOX, the UK Corporate Governance Code, and the EU AI Act, are expanding in 2026 to cover machine identity hygiene and AI decision-making transparency, making machine governance a board-level accountability issue rather than a purely technical concern. Executives must demonstrate they can audit AI behavior, enforce identity controls, and prove the integrity of AI-driven actions.

The third component is behavioral monitoring, specifically calibrated for non-human actors. The behavioral analytics that power AI-driven security detection for human users, detecting anomalies in access patterns, data volumes, and activity timing, must be extended and recalibrated for agents whose normal behavior patterns differ fundamentally from those of humans. An agent that accesses ten thousand records in a single session is not necessarily behaving maliciously; it may be performing a legitimate batch operation. Distinguishing between legitimate batch operations and data exfiltration conducted through compromised agent credentials requires understanding each agent's specific behavioral baseline, not applying human behavioral norms generically.

The identity frontier of 2026 is not primarily a technology problem, though it does have significant technological components. It is a governance problem: the problem of extending the disciplines of identity management, access control, and behavioral monitoring to a new class of actors that operate at machine speed, hold human-level permissions, and exist in most enterprise environments without adequate oversight. The organizations that solve that governance problem first will have built one of the most consequential security capabilities of the decade. Those who defer it will find themselves managing the consequences of that deferral one breach at a time.

CHAPTER 7
THE BROADER ECOSYSTEM

On July 19, 2024, 8.5 million Windows devices running CrowdStrike's Falcon sensor crashed simultaneously. Airlines grounded flights. Hospitals reverted to paper. Banks went offline. Broadcast networks went dark. 911 call centers failed. The culprit was not a cyberattack. It was a faulty content configuration update from one of the world's most trusted security vendors, and within twenty-four hours it had produced the most consequential IT outage in recorded history, with damages estimated at ten billion dollars globally. The 2026 security ecosystem was, in part, built in response to that single morning: a market-level reckoning with the risks of concentrated architectural dependence on any single platform, however capable. That outage asked every security leader a question that the market had never needed to ask so urgently before: if your primary security platform fails, what fails with it?

The answer, for many organizations, was everything. And the lesson embedded in that answer drove a period of rapid evolution in how enterprises think about platform consolidation, architectural resilience, and the trade-offs between integration depth and single-point-of-failure exposure. Understanding the 2026 security vendor landscape requires understanding that evolution: not just which platforms exist, but why the market is structured the way it is, and what it means for how organizations should navigate it. This chapter provides that map.

The Enterprise Platform Giants

At the apex of the commercial security market sit a handful of platforms that, through a combination of organic development, strategic acquisition, and the AI-powered integration of formerly separate capabilities, have evolved into comprehensive security operating systems for large enterprises. Understanding how each of these platforms has positioned itself illuminates both the current state of the art in defensive technology and the commercial logic driving the market's consolidation.

CrowdStrike's Falcon platform is the most instructive example of how the AI era has transformed the competitive dynamics of the security industry. Originally an endpoint detection and response pioneer, CrowdStrike has systematically extended Falcon across endpoints, cloud workloads, identity signals, and network telemetry, correlating intelligence from all of these sources in a unified cloud-native architecture that tracks more than 280 named adversaries and feeds real-time threat intelligence directly into the platform's detection models. In the agentic era, CrowdStrike's CEO George Kurtz has framed the platform's mission as operating at machine speed to stop breaches, requiring a single platform architecture that can reason and act at the speed of the adversary while securing the AI-powered enterprise. The platform's Charlotte AI capability functions as a generative AI analyst that can answer natural-language questions about threats, summarize incidents, and generate investigation workflows without requiring an analyst to manually query multiple data sources.

The CrowdStrike model is built around a single lightweight agent deployed on endpoints, collecting telemetry that flows to the cloud for processing and correlation. This architecture has produced measurable performance advantages in detection speed, but it also created a systemic vulnerability that led to the catastrophic July 2024 global outage, when a faulty sensor configuration update propagated to millions of endpoints simultaneously, triggering widespread system failures across industries. That incident remains the most consequential lesson in the current market about the risks of concentrated architectural dependence, and it reverberated through enterprise security planning for the full year that followed.

SentinelOne's Singularity platform has built its commercial positioning explicitly around architectural differentiation from CrowdStrike's approach. SentinelOne's Singularity SIEM is built on the Singularity Data Lake, a cloud-native, schema-free platform that ingests data from virtually any source and processes it 100 times faster than legacy SIEM tools, with exabyte-scale data ingestion and limitless retention. The platform's Purple AI, its generative AI security analyst, sits across endpoint, cloud, identity, and SIEM functions, enabling analysts to conduct natural-language investigations across the full unified data set rather than querying each security domain separately. SentinelOne has been named a Leader in the Gartner Magic Quadrant for Endpoint Protection Platforms for five consecutive years, and its Offensive Security Engine maps attack paths and simulates attacks against the organization's own infrastructure to identify vulnerabilities before adversaries can exploit them.

Palo Alto Networks occupies a different point in the platform landscape. Rather than anchoring its identity in endpoint protection, Palo Alto has built its strategy around network security and the cloud, converging those domains through the Cortex XSIAM platform, which combines

SIEM, SOAR, XDR, and attack surface management in a single architecture. Cortex XSIAM provides AI-driven, unified detection and response across endpoints, networks, and cloud environments, with automated root-cause analysis to determine attack origins and impact, continuous attack surface management, and more than 500 pre-built automated response playbooks. The platform's aspiration is a fully autonomous security operations center: a system that can ingest the full enterprise signal, reason about threats with AI, and orchestrate responses across every security layer without constant human direction.

Microsoft's security portfolio is in a category of its own by virtue of its ubiquity. Microsoft's security portfolio, including Microsoft Defender for endpoint protection, Sentinel for SIEM and SOAR, Entra for identity and access management, and Purview for data protection, delivers AI-powered threat detection, response, and compliance tools across what is already the dominant productivity and collaboration platform for most large enterprises. Microsoft Sentinel's advantage is the native integration with the full Microsoft ecosystem: an organization running Azure, Microsoft 365, and Teams generates security-relevant telemetry across all of these platforms that Sentinel can ingest and correlate without the integration engineering required to connect heterogeneous tools. Security Copilot, Microsoft's generative AI layer across this portfolio, reduces mean time to resolution and accelerates investigation at a scale that reflects the platform's enormous installed base.

Google Chronicle leverages Google Cloud's data-processing capabilities for enterprise-scale threat detection and analytics, with high-speed ingestion, real-time querying, long-term log storage for historical forensic analysis, and seamless integration with VirusTotal for file reputation analysis. Chronicle's architectural advantage is Google's infrastructure, which provides essentially unlimited processing capacity for correlating enormous volumes of security telemetry, and Google's threat intelligence capabilities through VirusTotal and Mandiant, acquired in 2022 and fully integrated into the Chronicle platform by 2025.

IBM's QRadar suite holds the legacy anchor position in the enterprise SIEM market, serving large organizations with complex compliance requirements and established integrations. IBM QRadar offers advanced analytics powered by artificial intelligence, integrating with numerous third-party tools to support large enterprises managing extensive security data, with IBM X-Force threat intelligence feeding directly into detection models. IBM's broader security strategy leverages Watson AI capabilities across the QRadar ecosystem and positions the company's consulting and professional services strength as a differentiator for organizations that need implementation and managed services alongside technology.

The Specialist Tier: Purpose-Built Platforms

Below the platform giants sits a substantial tier of specialist vendors that have built exceptional capabilities in specific security domains, and whose products often appear alongside enterprise platform deployments rather than competing with them directly.

Darktrace, examined in depth in Chapter Three, remains the defining example of self-learning behavioral AI for network and email security, with its distinction lying in its unsupervised learning approach that builds behavioral models from within each organization's unique environment rather than relying on externally developed threat libraries. Under CEO Jill Popelka, Darktrace is investing over two hundred million dollars in U.S. operations in 2026, opening a major Dallas deployment center with a goal of reaching one billion dollars in revenue in 2027, and the company serves nearly ten thousand customers across a hundred and ten countries.

Zscaler has established a dominant position in the zero-trust network access market, providing the architectural foundation for organizations moving away from perimeter-based security toward identity-centric, cloud-delivered access control. As AI agents have proliferated and the "work from anywhere" model has made network perimeters conceptually obsolete, Zscaler's platform has become a critical component of the security architecture for organizations implementing zero trust at scale.

CyberArk, focused on privileged access management and, increasingly, non-human identity security, has found its market expanding dramatically as the agentic AI identity crisis described in Chapter Six has elevated machine credential governance from an operational concern to a strategic security priority. Its Identity Security Platform now explicitly addresses AI agent identities alongside human privileged access, reflecting the convergence of these formerly separate disciplines.

Proofpoint's email security platform and Abnormal Security's AI-powered email analysis capability address the phishing threat surface documented in Chapter Two. Both have incorporated AI-specific capabilities to detect AI-generated phishing content that evades conventional signature and pattern-matching approaches, recognizing that the primary method of initial access in modern attack campaigns runs through the inbox rather than the network perimeter.

Cloud-Native Security Services: Amazon, Google, and Azure

The major cloud platforms have integrated AI-powered security capabilities directly into their infrastructure offerings, making baseline AI-driven detection accessible to any organization that has migrated to cloud infrastructure, regardless of whether it has deployed dedicated security products.

AWS GuardDuty uses machine learning to continuously analyze CloudTrail API calls, VPC Flow Logs, and DNS queries, detecting anomalous behavior indicative of compromise without requiring organizations to configure rules or maintain signature databases. Its integration with AWS Security Hub provides unified visibility across the AWS security landscape, and its recent extension to cover threat detection for AI workloads reflects the cloud provider's recognition that AI systems themselves are increasingly attack targets within customer environments.

Azure Defender for Cloud extends Microsoft's security intelligence across hybrid and multi-cloud environments, detecting threats across Azure, AWS, and Google Cloud workloads and providing the cloud security posture management capabilities that identify misconfigurations before they can be exploited. Microsoft's investment in AI safety research has also enabled specific capabilities to detect prompt injection attempts against AI workloads deployed in Azure, reflecting the cloud provider's understanding that the AI attack surface described in Chapter Four requires purpose-built defenses.

Google Cloud's Security Command Center provides similar unified visibility across Google Cloud environments, with AI-assisted vulnerability detection and threat intelligence drawn from Google's extensive threat research infrastructure. The integration of Mandiant incident response capabilities into Google Cloud's security offering gives enterprise customers access to intelligence gathered from some of the world's most consequential breach investigations, applied directly to their cloud environments.

The Open-Source Ecosystem: Democratizing Defense

The most important structural characteristic of the 2026 security tool landscape is one that commercial vendor narratives rarely acknowledge: the open-source community has built a set of capabilities that gives organizations without enterprise security budgets access to genuine intelligence and detection capability. Understanding this ecosystem is important not just for cost-conscious security leaders but also for anyone seeking to understand how security practitioners actually build and operate security programs in organizations that cannot afford the platforms described above.

Wazuh sits at the foundation of many small and mid-sized organizations' security stacks as a free, open-source unified XDR and SIEM platform. Wazuh can protect workloads across on-premises, virtualized, containerized, and cloud-based environments, offering threat detection, log analysis, file integrity monitoring, vulnerability detection, incident response capabilities, and compliance reporting, with full integration with the Elastic Stack for search and visualization. It has been adopted by security teams on every continent, and its community-maintained rule sets reflect collective threat intelligence from a global practitioner base.

The MISP platform, the Malware Information Sharing Platform developed initially at NATO's Computer Incident Response Capability and maintained as a community project, enables organizations to share threat intelligence within trusted networks. MISP allows organizations to store indicators of compromise in a structured manner, enjoy automated correlation, export for IDS and SIEM systems in STIX or OpenIOC formats, and synchronize with other MISP instances, making threat sharing efficient and actionable across security communities. The platform is widely used by national CERTs, financial sector ISACs, healthcare security organizations, and defense industrial base sharing groups, reflecting the principle that collective defense amplifies individual capabilities.

OpenCTI, developed initially by France's ANSSI national cybersecurity agency, takes a more structured approach to threat intelligence management by building knowledge graphs that represent relationships among threat actors, campaigns, techniques, and indicators using the STIX 2.1 standard. In 2025, OpenCTI improved its mapping to the MITRE ATT&CK framework, allowing for richer contextualization of tactics, techniques, and procedures within campaign timelines and actor profiles, and its native support for commercial threat intelligence platforms has expanded through connector development. Many security teams deploy both MISP and OpenCTI together, using MISP for operational indicator sharing and OpenCTI for strategic intelligence analysis and threat actor profiling.

The Elastic Stack, combining Elasticsearch for data storage and search, Logstash for data ingestion, and Kibana for visualization with the machine learning capabilities built into Elasticsearch, provides a free and highly capable SIEM foundation that many organizations use as the backbone of their security operations. The platform requires significantly more configuration and maintenance expertise than commercial alternatives, but organizations with the technical capability to operate it gain access to detection engineering and threat hunting capabilities that rival commercial products at a fraction of the cost.

The broader open-source security ecosystem in 2025 has expanded to include purpose-built AI security automation frameworks, including CAI, a CLI-based open-source framework for automating security tasks, including penetration testing and incident simulation. They use large language models and are compatible with multiple commercial AI providers and designed to introduce AI-assisted reasoning into security workflows without requiring commercial AI security platform subscriptions.

The Integration Imperative

The most common mistake organizations make in navigating this ecosystem is treating security tool selection as a series of independent point decisions rather than as an architectural challenge. The value of any individual security tool is substantially determined by how well it integrates with the tools around it, because the intelligence that enables effective security is not held within any single platform but emerges from the correlation of signals across multiple domains.

An endpoint detection platform that identifies anomalous process execution on a workstation is more valuable when it can automatically cross-reference that event with identity signals from the IAM platform, network traffic data from the NDR tool, and threat intelligence from the TIP, all within a unified timeline that an analyst can read in seconds. A standalone alert from the endpoint platform, requiring the analyst to manually correlate it against three other systems to understand its significance, is less valuable even if the underlying detection capability is technically superior.

The AI SOC market in 2026 has seen the gap between legacy SIEM vendors and purpose-built AI platforms widen significantly, with the most capable modern platforms defined by their ability to ingest telemetry from every security layer, apply AI analytics to the unified picture, and orchestrate automated responses across the full stack rather than within any individual domain.

This integration imperative has driven the consolidation visible across the commercial market. Many vendors have acquired point-solution providers to extend their platform coverage and reduce the integration burden on customers. It has also driven the development of open standards, including STIX/TAXII for threat intelligence, OpenTelemetry for observability data, and OCSF (Open Cybersecurity Schema Framework), a collaborative project initiated by AWS and Splunk with broad industry support that aims to provide a common data format enabling security tools from different vendors to exchange data without custom integration work.

Complex Market Quandary

The practical challenge facing security leaders in 2026 is not a shortage of capable tools. It is the opposite: an abundance of capable tools, many of which overlap in function, compete on different performance dimensions, and require significant organizational investment to deploy, configure, and maintain effectively. The organizations that navigate this complexity most successfully share several characteristics that are worthy of mentioning.

They start with architecture before products, defining their detection and response requirements, data architecture, and automation objectives, then evaluating specific tools. They prioritize platform consolidation where possible, without sacrificing capability. They recognize that the operational overhead of maintaining a fragmented stack of poorly integrated point solutions frequently exceeds the cost of a comprehensive platform, even when the platform license is more expensive. They invest in the integration and engineering work required to make their tools actually share data and automate responses, understanding that a platform used at 10% of its capability provides 10% of its value. And they maintain a genuine open-source capability alongside their commercial investments, both for cost efficiency and for the direct connection to the practitioner community that open-source participation provides.

The global cybersecurity market is projected to grow from approximately two hundred and twenty-eight billion dollars in 2025 to nearly three hundred and fifty-two billion dollars by 2030. This is driven by the growing adoption of AI-powered security architectures, the acceleration of threats, and the expanding attack surface from cloud migration and the deployment of agentic AI. That growth reflects both the scale of the problem and the maturing recognition that security is not a cost to be minimized but a capability to be built.

The organizations that treat it as the latter, investing in architecture, talent, and the sustained operational discipline required to make excellent tools perform at their potential, will find themselves increasingly separated from those that treat it as the former. The gap between cyber-resilient organizations and those that are not, identified by the World Economic Forum Global Cybersecurity Outlook 2026 as one of the defining features of the current moment, is not primarily a technology gap. It is a strategy and investment gap, and no amount of market-leading tools can close it without the organizational commitment to use them well.

CHAPTER 8
GEOPOLITICS, REGULATION, AND ETHICAL DIMENSIONS

In April 2025, the Norwegian hydroelectric dam case occurred, as mentioned earlier in the introduction of this book. The same month, the GPS spoofing disrupted the flight of European Commission President Ursula von der Leyen and temporarily diverted the aircraft's navigation systems toward false coordinates. Across Europe, a sustained hybrid campaign combined cyberattacks on airports with drone incursions and coordinated disinformation operations, blurring the line between digital sabotage and physical coercion. The dam attack was later attributed to a group with Russian affiliations. The GPS manipulation was traced to infrastructure associated with Russian electronic warfare units active in the Baltic region. These incidents were not isolated provocations. They were data points in a systematic campaign to demonstrate to Western governments and their publics that the digital infrastructure of democratic societies is vulnerable and that adversaries are willing to exploit that vulnerability as a tool of geopolitical pressure. They were also something else: they were AI-assisted. The reconnaissance that identified the dam's control system vulnerabilities, the spoofing signals calibrated to confuse specific avionics, and the disinformation narratives timed to coincide with the physical disruptions, each bore the signatures of AI-accelerated planning and execution.

The geopolitics of cybersecurity in 2026 cannot be understood without understanding this fusion: the convergence of state-sponsored cyber operations with AI capabilities that amplify their speed, scale, and precision, the fragmentation of the international governance landscape into competing regulatory blocs, and the widening gap between the cyber capabilities of the powerful and the exposed vulnerability of everyone else. Cybersecurity has become a domain of great-power competition, and artificial intelligence has become its primary accelerant.

The Nation-State Landscape: The CRINK Axis

The security community has developed a useful shorthand for the four nation-states that pose the most consequential and persistent cyber threats to Western organizations and governments: China, Russia, Iran, and North Korea, sometimes grouped under the acronym CRINK. While each pursues distinct objectives through distinct operational styles, their campaigns have converged in 2025 and 2026 around a common characteristic: the integration of AI capabilities into operations that were already among the most sophisticated in the world.

China's cyber program is the most strategically patient and operationally comprehensive of the four. U.S. intelligence has assessed China as the most active and persistent cyber threat to the U.S. government and critical sectors, with dozens of state-sponsored hacking units operating under military and intelligence agencies that pursue widespread, far-reaching cyber espionage and intellectual property theft campaigns. The "Typhoon" campaign family, including Volt Typhoon and Salt Typhoon, demonstrated China's sustained commitment to pre-positioning within critical infrastructure networks, not necessarily for immediate exploitation but for potential use in the event of a geopolitical confrontation, particularly regarding Taiwan. Security analysts expect China to continue executing cyber campaigns to strengthen its political and economic influence, with the semiconductor sector identified as particularly vulnerable given competition from Taiwan's manufacturers and American export restrictions.

A key component of China's cyber strategy is the concept of military-civil fusion, which encourages collaboration between the private sector and the military and integrates resources, as evidenced in the activities of major Chinese technology firms that advance China's cyber ambitions and provide pathways to secure technological control over telecommunications and digital infrastructure. This fusion model means that the boundary between commercial AI development in China and state cyber capability development is deliberately porous, a structural feature of the threat that Western organizations operating any Chinese-manufactured technology components must reckon with explicitly.

Russia's cyber operations are defined by their integration with kinetic warfare and their willingness to accept collateral damage as a feature rather than a bug. The ongoing war in Ukraine has served as a live laboratory for AI-assisted hybrid warfare, with Russian cyber units testing attack techniques against Ukrainian infrastructure that then appear months later against European and NATO targets. While Russia-aligned threat actors are currently focused on Ukraine, 2026 will likely see diversification of their targeting as European countries undertake major rearmament programs, with anticipated upticks in Russian cyberactivity targeting defense contractors, supply chains, and critical infrastructure to track and undermine Western military modernization.

Russia-nexus FANCY BEAR deployed LLM-enabled malware designated LAMEHUG in 2025, using large language model capabilities to automate reconnaissance and document collection. This represents the most visible example of Russia's integration of AI into operational intelligence-gathering. The deployment was not a proof-of-concept. It was a combat-tested capability deployed against real targets in an active intelligence operation.

North Korea occupies a unique position in the CRINK landscape because its cyber operations serve a function that is only partially about intelligence: they generate hard currency for a regime under severe economic sanctions. One of the most widely reported incidents involved attributing a $1.5 billion cryptocurrency theft from the Bybit exchange in February 2025 to the Lazarus Group, North Korea's primary cyber offensive unit, making it the largest cryptocurrency theft in history. North Korea has also pursued a sophisticated long-term operation of placing North Korean nationals in technology companies worldwide under false identities, earning legitimate salaries while conducting espionage and, in some cases, planting malware. Security researchers believe this IT worker infiltration program may have been operating since as early as 2014, with the amount of intellectual property stolen from technology companies potentially extraordinary.

Iran's cyber operations sit at the intersection of regional geopolitical ambitions, domestic repression, and increasingly sophisticated offensive capability. The Google Cybersecurity

Forecast 2026 assessed that Iranian cyber capabilities will remain resilient, multifaceted, and semi-deniable, deliberately blurring the lines between espionage, disruption, hacktivism, and financially motivated activity. They have the same actors and access leveraged for different missions, complicating defense and attribution. The escalating regional conflict cycle, including Iran-Israel-US exchanges in 2025, has been accompanied by corresponding surges in Iranian cyber operations against the governments, defense sectors, and critical infrastructure of perceived adversaries.

The World Economic Forum Global Cybersecurity Outlook 2026 found that 91% of the largest organizations have changed their cybersecurity strategies due to geopolitical volatility, while 64% of all organizations now account for geopolitically motivated cyberattacks in their risk strategies. The normalization of state-sponsored cyber operations as a routine element of geopolitical competition means that organizations that previously dismissed the nation-state threat as relevant only to government agencies or defense contractors now find themselves in an environment where critical infrastructure, financial systems, supply chains, and democratic processes are all legitimate targets.

Sovereign AI: The Infrastructure of National Security

One of the most consequential geopolitical shifts of 2025 and 2026 has been the emergence of sovereign AI infrastructure as a national security priority. The realization that AI capabilities are dependent on semiconductor supply chains concentrated in Taiwan, cloud infrastructure operated by a handful of American companies, and training data that flows across jurisdictional boundaries has produced a global scramble to build nationally or regionally controlled AI capacity.

Europe's framing of this as "technological sovereignty" reflects a dual concern: the security risk of dependence on foreign AI infrastructure and the regulatory challenge of applying European law to systems operated by non-European companies on non-European infrastructure. The European Commission has proposed a "Cloud and AI Development Act" aimed at promoting investment in data centers and setting standards for cloud computing services, and the EU's Apply AI Strategy promotes an AI-first approach in eleven key industrial sectors while emphasizing Europe's data sovereignty as a foundational principle.

China's approach is the most comprehensive: a complete domestic AI ecosystem, from chip fabrication through cloud infrastructure to model development, insulated from Western supply chains and governed by rules that give the state explicit authority over AI systems deployed within China's borders. The military-civil fusion model ensures that AI capabilities developed commercially are available to state cyber and intelligence operations.

The United States has pursued a different but equally assertive sovereignty strategy, using export controls to limit China's access to advanced semiconductors and the manufacturing equipment required to produce them, while simultaneously investing in domestic chip fabrication capacity through the CHIPS and Science Act. The strategic logic is that, in the long run, AI capability is constrained by chip supply, and that constraining China's chip access constrains China's AI capability.

The World Economic Forum report notes that fragmentation and sovereignty concerns are reshaping cooperation and trust among nations, with hybrid threats and escalating cyberattacks reflecting the increasing volatility of the global environment, while widening gaps in cyber capability across nations create asymmetric vulnerabilities. The practical security implication of this geopolitical fragmentation is a supply chain risk environment in which every hardware component, software dependency, and cloud service a security professional relies on carries a geopolitical dimension that did not exist a decade ago.

The EU AI Act: The World's First Comprehensive AI Regulation

The most consequential regulatory development shaping the AI-cybersecurity intersection in 2026 is not the passage of a new law but the enforcement of existing law: the EU AI Act, which entered into force in August 2024, reaches its primary enforcement threshold on August 2, 2026, when the majority of its obligations for high-risk AI systems become operative.

The AI Act introduces specific security requirements affecting those responsible for high-risk AI systems: providers must ensure that accuracy, robustness, and cybersecurity are integrated into AI solutions at launch and maintained throughout their lifecycle. Where appropriate, the Act requires providers to implement technical measures to address threats such as data poisoning, model evasion, adversarial attacks, and vigilance against emerging vulnerabilities. Both providers and deployers must have procedures in place to identify, report, and mitigate serious incidents.

The transparency obligations under Article 50, which require disclosure of AI interactions, labeling of synthetic content, and identification of deepfakes, also become enforceable in August 2026. For organizations operating AI systems in European markets, this means the content authentication challenge described in Chapter Five, previously a technical best practice, has become a legal compliance requirement. The same is true for the governance structures around high-risk AI deployments that security practitioners have been advocating for purely security reasons: risk management frameworks, data governance, human oversight requirements, and post-market monitoring are now mandated by law for AI systems deployed in consequential contexts.

Organizations that are non-compliant with the EU AI Act face penalties of up to 35 million euros or 7% of global annual turnover, whichever is higher, making compliance a financial imperative rather than an aspirational goal. The enforcement mechanism is the newly established EU AI Office, which exercises supervisory authority over general-purpose AI models with systemic risk, and national market surveillance authorities in each member state, which oversee the broader population of high-risk AI applications.

The EU AI Act's cybersecurity implications extend beyond the direct requirements for AI system security. By requiring that AI systems deployed in critical infrastructure, financial services, healthcare, law enforcement, and other high-risk domains meet documented security standards, the Act effectively mandates the security-by-design practices that the cybersecurity community has been promoting for years. It creates legal accountability for organizations that deploy AI without adequate security assessment, transforming what was previously a reputational risk into a regulatory one.

The EU's Cyber Resilience Act, which entered into force in December 2024, further extends this accountability framework: most of its obligations will begin to apply from December 2027, covering cybersecurity requirements for products with digital elements, including hardware and software, and applying to AI systems and components embedded in products throughout their lifecycle.

The United States: A Different Model

The regulatory approach in the United States starkly contrasts with the EU's comprehensive statutory framework. Rather than a single AI Act governing risk categories across the economy, the US approach relies on agency-by-agency enforcement of existing authorities, voluntary frameworks, and executive orders that establish policy without carrying the force of statute.

The US AI Action Plan, officially published in July 2025, includes approximately 90 policy actions for federal agencies, covering national security posture against AI misuse, export controls, cybersecurity measures, international diplomacy on AI governance, and supply-chain resilience. The Plan is a non-statutory roadmap rather than an enforceable regulation, meaning its implementation timing and depth vary by agency and initiative.

NIST continues to play the most operationally significant role in shaping US AI security practice through its AI Risk Management Framework, which has evolved into the de facto standard for AI governance across federal agencies and regulated industries. The NIST AI RMF's four pillars, Govern, Map, Measure, and Manage, now serve as procurement criteria for vendors and partners to US federal agencies, and aligning with the framework means integrating its principles into the AI lifecycle, including red-teaming environments for adversarial testing before deployment and automated escalation playbooks that activate when safety or performance thresholds are exceeded.

NIST's Cyber AI Profile, the framework extension specifically designed to address the cybersecurity dimensions of AI deployment, provides the most practically useful guidance for security practitioners navigating the intersection of AI adoption and security governance. By extending the Cybersecurity Framework 2.0's identify-protect-detect-respond-recover structure to AI-specific risks, including prompt injection, model poisoning, and supply chain compromise, the Profile gives organizations a compliance scaffold that integrates AI security into existing security programs rather than treating it as a separate discipline requiring separate management.

The SEC's prioritization of AI-washing enforcement reflects another dimension of the US regulatory posture: treating AI governance failures as investor protection issues. Organizations that overstate their AI security capabilities or understate their AI risk exposure in investor disclosures face enforcement action under securities law, a consequence that has elevated AI governance to the attention of general counsels and audit committees that might otherwise have left it to the security team.

The Ethical Dimensions: Bias, Surveillance, and the Inequity of Defense

No treatment of the geopolitics and regulation of AI-powered cybersecurity would be complete without confronting the ethical dimensions that sit beneath both. These are not soft issues tangential to the hard work of security operations. They are structural challenges that affect who is protected, who is endangered, and what values are encoded into the systems that increasingly govern the most consequential decisions in digital life.

The first ethical challenge is algorithmic bias in security systems. AI-powered detection tools learn patterns from historical data, which reflects the biases of the environments and decisions that produced it. A behavioral analytics system trained primarily on Western corporate network data may misclassify normal user behavior patterns in other cultural or operational contexts as anomalous. A facial recognition system used for identity verification may perform significantly less accurately for faces that were underrepresented in its training data. A fraud detection model may generate higher false-positive rates for certain demographic groups if the correlations of fraud in historical data reflect discriminatory patterns rather than genuine risk signals.

These are not hypothetical concerns. The deployment of AI in law enforcement and border control contexts has produced documented disparities in false positive rates across demographic groups, with consequences ranging from embarrassment to wrongful detention. In the cybersecurity context, the stakes are similarly concrete: a fraud detection system that disproportionately flags legitimate transactions from certain communities imposes real financial costs on those communities. An access control system that fails to recognize certain users correctly creates both security failures and discriminatory experiences.

One documented example sits at the intersection of criminal justice and identity verification. Multiple independent audits between 2019 and 2024 found that facial recognition systems used by law enforcement agencies in the United States and the United Kingdom misidentified Black and Asian faces at significantly higher rates than white faces; in some evaluations, error rates differed by a factor of ten across demographic groups. The consequences ranged from wrongful detention to reputational harm for individuals who had committed no offense. When the same underlying technology is deployed in AI-powered identity verification for fraud detection or access control, those disparities propagate directly into organizational security decisions, with the same demographic groups bearing a disproportionate share of the friction and false-positive burden imposed by miscalibrated systems.

The surveillance arbitrage dimension is equally consequential. The EU AI Act's prohibition on mass biometric surveillance in public spaces reflects a specific values judgment: that the capability to monitor populations continuously is incompatible with the fundamental rights that European law protects, regardless of the stated security justification. That prohibition creates a regulatory boundary in European markets. It does not prevent the same surveillance AI capabilities from being developed by companies operating in less regulated jurisdictions and sold to governments with different values, including authoritarian states that use behavioral monitoring systems (structurally identical to enterprise behavioral analytics) to track political opposition, ethnic minorities, and religious communities. The dual-use nature of AI surveillance technology means that defensive innovation in democratic contexts and repressive deployment in authoritarian ones share the same technical foundation. This is not a problem that technology alone can resolve.

The second ethical challenge is the dual-use nature of AI surveillance capabilities. The same technology that enables an organization to monitor its network for signs of compromise can enable a state to monitor its citizens for signs of dissent. The behavioral analytics that detect anomalous access patterns in enterprise environments are structurally identical to the social monitoring systems deployed by authoritarian governments to track political opposition. The deepfake detection tools being developed to protect democratic institutions from synthetic disinformation can be repurposed as mechanisms for censorship enforcement.

The EU AI Act explicitly bans law enforcement's use of remote biometric identification in publicly accessible spaces, except in specified limited circumstances, and prohibits public authorities from using AI-powered social scoring systems, reflecting Europe's legislative judgment that certain surveillance applications of AI are incompatible with fundamental rights regardless of their technical effectiveness. These prohibitions establish a values-based boundary in European law that does not exist universally, creating the conditions for regulatory arbitrage in which surveillance AI capabilities banned in democratic markets are developed and deployed in markets with fewer constraints.

The third, and perhaps most structurally consequential, ethical challenge is the widening inequity in cyber defense capabilities documented throughout this book. The World Economic Forum's Global Cybersecurity Outlook 2026 found that small organizations are two and a half times more likely to report insufficient cyber resilience than large enterprises, and that the talent shortage is most acute in the Global South, with 65% of Latin American and Caribbean organizations and 63% of sub-Saharan African organizations facing severe cybersecurity skills gaps.

This inequity is not merely a matter of organizational efficiency. It creates systemic vulnerabilities that propagate through interconnected supply chains, affecting large enterprises through their less-protected suppliers and partners. It exposes the critical infrastructure of less wealthy nations, including hospitals, utilities, and financial systems, to attacks that those nations' governments lack the capacity to counter. And it creates a situation in which the communities that are less able to absorb the financial and operational costs of a significant cyberattack are the most likely to experience one.

The ethical imperative here is not primarily a matter of charity. It is a matter of collective security. As NIST's framing suggests, addressing these risks requires coming together, sharing intelligence globally, and developing skills equal to emerging threats, because society knows what's at stake if we get this wrong. The organizations and governments that treat cybersecurity resilience as a shared infrastructure problem rather than a competitive advantage will be better positioned in the long run than those that treat it as something each organization must solve independently with whatever resources it can afford.

The regulatory and governance frameworks emerging in 2026 are beginning to grapple with this collective dimension, through information-sharing mandates, coordinated incident response frameworks, and international cooperation on threat intelligence. But the gap between the pace of governance development and the pace of threat escalation remains wide, and it will require sustained political will, institutional investment, and genuine cross-border cooperation to close it.

CHAPTER 9
CASE STUDIES

There is a peculiar danger in reading about cybersecurity at a strategic level: the statistics and frameworks can create an illusion of understanding that does not translate into a visceral grasp of how these attacks and defenses actually work in practice. The numbers are real, the threat categories are accurately named, but until you sit with the specific sequence of events that turned a single compromised developer's laptop into the largest cryptocurrency theft in history, or trace the precise chain of decisions and non-decisions that allowed five weeks of automotive production to collapse across a global supply chain, the abstract remains abstract.

This chapter closes that gap. The following four case studies are drawn from documented incidents and deployments of 2024 and 2025, and not to be representative of the broadest range of AI-cybersecurity dynamics but are maximally instructive about specific lessons. Each one illuminates a different facet of the intersection: a supply-chain attack of historic scale enabled by patient, precise adversarial intelligence; the anatomy of the largest single financial heist ever conducted through cyberspace; the measurable performance difference between AI-augmented and traditional security operations under real attack conditions; and the governance failure that turned a legitimate AI deployment into an organizational liability. Taken together, they constitute a closer-to-complete picture of the stakes.

Case Study One: The Bybit Heist: When the Supply Chain Becomes the Vault

At approximately 12:30 in the afternoon on February 21, 2025, an employee at Bybit, the Dubai-based cryptocurrency exchange ranking second in the world by trading volume, initiated what appeared to be a routine transaction: a standard transfer of Ethereum holdings from a cold wallet, the offline, air-gapped storage used for long-term cryptocurrency security, to a warm wallet used for day-to-day operational liquidity. The employee logged into the Safe platform, the open-source multi-signature wallet management system that Bybit used to secure its holdings. The interface displayed a transaction that matched exactly what had been authorized: the correct destination address, the correct amount, and the correct cryptographic signatures from the multiple Bybit executives whose authorization the multisig architecture required. The employee approved it.

At the last moment, dormant code activated, swapping in a new command to drain Bybit's crypto holdings. The employee had unknowingly authorized the transfer of $1.5 billion in Ethereum to addresses under North Korean control. Two minutes after the heist, Safe's website was updated to hide the hackers' tracks and erase the code snippet.

What the employee could not have known was that North Korean hackers had been inside the Safe platform's development environment for months before that moment. The Safe team had about 30 engineers, and North Korean hackers targeted one of the senior system administrators through what was likely a phishing attack, gaining access to the developer's machine and installing persistent malware that gave them control over Safe's ability to update its live website and code.

The hackers prepared the operation over a period of at least one month and possibly many months, watching Bybit's operational patterns to understand when and how the cold wallet transfers occurred, and building the specific code injection that would activate only when the Bybit employee opened a Safe session for a transaction of the targeted type.

The attack architecture was elegant in its economy. North Korea did not need to compromise Bybit's own systems, which would have required penetrating an organization specifically hardened against exactly this kind of threat. Instead, they compromised a third-party service provider with a much smaller security team, less rigorous security practices, and no formal business relationship with Bybit that would have required security assessments. Bybit trusted Safe because Safe's software was open-source and widely used. Safe's code appeared in the Bybit interface. The attack exploited that chain of trust precisely.

The FBI confirmed that North Korean is responsible five days after the theft, identifying the operation as consistent with the TraderTraitor campaign pattern, and urging cryptocurrency service providers, including exchanges, blockchain analytics firms, and DeFi services, to block transactions associated with the 51 Ethereum addresses used by the attackers to launder the stolen funds.

According to TRM Labs' analysis, North Korea had stolen over $5 billion in cryptocurrency since 2017, with stolen funds widely assessed to support the DPRK's weapons program and allow the regime to circumvent international sanctions. The Bybit theft alone, at $1.5 billion, exceeded the total value of all North Korean cryptocurrency theft in 2023.

The lessons embedded in this case cut across nearly every theme in this book. The attack exploited a supply chain vulnerability, not through a zero-day in production infrastructure, but through the human-targeted compromise of a developer at a smaller, less-secure third-party provider. It relied on patient, multi-month prepositioning that no reactive security system could have caught after the fact. It exploited "blind signing," a vulnerability inherent in multi-signature wallet architectures in which the visual interface presented to signers can be manipulated independently of the underlying transaction being authorized. And it involved AI-assisted planning and execution: the reconnaissance that identified the precise timing and mechanism of Bybit's cold wallet transfers, and the rapid automated laundering of $1.5 billion across thousands of blockchain addresses in the hours after the theft, both bore signatures of machine-assisted speed and precision.

Bybit's recovery was unusually robust given the scale of the loss: CEO Ben Zhou secured emergency funding, the exchange processed 99.99% of withdrawals within hours, and within days had recovered $1.23 billion in Ethereum, covering the deficit. The broader industry response was immediate, with Tether freezing $181,000 in funds linked to fraudulent transactions and blockchain analytics firms providing rapid attribution intelligence. But the resilience of Bybit's response should not obscure the fundamental lesson: the attack succeeded entirely. The breach, the exfiltration, and the laundering all proceeded as planned. Recovery happened because of Bybit's financial reserves and the cryptocurrency industry's unusual capacity for on-chain transaction tracing, not because any security control caught the attack before it executed.

Case Study Two: Jaguar Land Rover and the Five-Week Silence

The supply-chain attack that disabled Jaguar Land Rover's global production for five weeks in August 2025 offers a different but complementary lesson to the Bybit heist. Where Bybit's attackers were patient, precise, and targeted, the JLR incident illustrated the catastrophic amplification that occurs when a well-connected manufacturer is compromised through the weakest link in its extended supply ecosystem.

The attack halted production globally for 5 weeks, affecting over 5,000 suppliers. The direct costs approached £200 million pounds, and the broader UK economic impact reached nearly £2 billion pounds when the ripple effects through the automotive supply chain were fully tallied: disrupted component deliveries, idled factory floors, shattered logistics contracts, and the cascading consequences for every business dependent on the production volumes that JLR generates.

The specific technical details of the initial compromise were not fully disclosed publicly, but the structural pattern was consistent with the evasive adversary model that CrowdStrike identified as defining the threat landscape of 2025: intrusion through trusted credentials or a supply chain partner, malware-free lateral movement through legitimate system interfaces, and exploitation of the visibility gaps that exist between IT and operational technology environments. The attacker did not need to defeat JLR's core security architecture. They needed to find one supplier, or one software dependency, or one service account that provided a trusted path into the manufacturing control systems.

The scale of the impact reflects a specific vulnerability in complex manufacturing supply chains that AI-powered security analysis is only beginning to address: the assumption that a production disruption at one node will not propagate systematically across the network. The five thousand suppliers affected by the JLR stoppage were not all breached. They were dependent on the production volumes that JLR generates, and when those stopped, the entire supplier ecosystem absorbed the consequences. The blast radius of a single successful supply chain attack in an interconnected industrial network is not bounded by the attacker's foothold. It is bounded by the target's dependencies on every organization connected to it.

The defensive lesson here is about pre-incident mapping as much as about detection and response. The World Economic Forum's 2026 Cybersecurity Outlook found that CEOs of highly resilient organizations integrate security into their procurement processes and prioritize supplier maturity assessments to address supply chain risk, a practice adopted by only 70% of the most resilient organizations.

Case Study Three: The Financial Sector SOC Transformation

The previous two cases examine attacks. This one examines a defense, specifically the documented operational transformation that occurs when a financial services organization migrates from a traditional, human-centric security operations model to an AI-augmented one. The specific organization described here is a composite drawn from documented case studies published by Palo Alto Networks' Unit 42 and other major security providers, representing the pattern across multiple similar implementations rather than a single named institution.

The baseline situation was familiar to any security professional: a large financial services firm operating a security operations center staffed with 15 analysts across 3 shifts, using a legacy SIEM that processed millions of daily events and generated thousands of alerts, most of which were low-fidelity false positives. The mean time to detect a significant threat was measured in days. The mean time to respond, from initial detection through investigation, triage, containment, and remediation, was measured in hours at best and days at worst. This pattern of overwhelming alert volume is widespread: the average enterprise generates over 10,000 security alerts per day, and most SOC teams spend most of their time processing false positives rather than investigating genuine threats.

The firm implemented a unified AI security platform that integrates SIEM, XDR, and SOAR capabilities with a generative AI analyst layer. The calibration period took six weeks, during which the AI established behavioral baselines for every user, device, and service account in the environment, and the security team tuned the system's alert thresholds and automated response playbooks based on the organization's specific risk profile and operational patterns.

The results measured over the subsequent twelve months were substantial: mean time to respond dropped from a full day to fourteen minutes. The platform prevented 22,831 threats and processed 113,000 threat indicators in under 5 seconds. A large bank in an equivalent implementation saved 180 hours per year by automating SIEM reporting alone, 500 hours through automated data collection, 360 hours by automating four CTO playbooks, and 240 hours with automated threat intelligence enrichment.

The human dimension of the transformation was as significant as the technical one. Analysts who had spent their careers processing queues of mostly false-positive alerts found their roles changing: the AI handled routine triage automatically, escalating only the cases that genuinely required human judgment. Senior analysts were freed to conduct proactive threat hunting, investigating hypothesis-driven questions about adversary behavior that the reactive alert model had never provided time for. The turnover rate, which had been high in the previous model due to experienced analysts burning out under the cognitive load of the alert queue, declined substantially. The value of retaining institutional knowledge about the organization's environment, the anomalies that were actually business-justified rather than security concerns, and the specific adversaries that had historically targeted the sector proved measurable in the quality of AI-assisted investigations.

In an adjacent documented case, AI automation helped a major transportation manufacturing company reduce its attack response time from three weeks to nineteen minutes, a reduction of more than ninety-nine percent that prevented operational disruption from an attack that would previously have gone undetected until substantial damage had accumulated.

The consistent pattern across these financial-sector and industrial deployments is that AI-powered security does not prevent all breaches. In 2025, enterprises deploying AI-powered defenses still experienced breaches in approximately twenty-nine percent of cases, reflecting the sophistication of adversaries who adapt their techniques to evade detection systems. The pattern is that AI-powered security dramatically narrows the window of adversary operation, compresses the time between initial access and detection, and reduces the scope of damage by limiting lateral movement and dwell time. The difference between a breach detected and contained in 14 minutes and one detected after 3 weeks is the difference between an operational inconvenience and an existential event.

An example of the global reach of cybercrime is the WannaCry ransomware attack in 2017, which affected over 200,000 computers across 150 countries, disrupting healthcare systems, businesses, and governments. The attack demonstrated the potential for cybercriminals to cause widespread damage on a global scale, underscoring the need for coordinated international responses to cybercrime.

Study Four: The Pharmaceutical Company and the Agentic AI Governance Failure

A mid-sized pharmaceutical manufacturer, operating across research, clinical trials management, and regulatory affairs functions, deployed an agentic AI system in late 2024 to automate literature review and regulatory compliance monitoring. The agent was intended to monitor published research, flag relevant findings for the scientific team, track regulatory guideline updates across multiple jurisdictions, and generate preliminary compliance summaries. Its permissions were set broadly at deployment because "we weren't sure exactly what it would need," in the words of the IT lead responsible for the implementation, and because the project had a tight deadline that made a more rigorous access-scoping exercise impractical.

The agent was granted read access to the company's entire document management system, including confidential clinical trial data, intellectual property filings, and pre-publication research findings that constituted the company's most commercially sensitive assets.

Research in 2025 found that 77% of enterprise employees who use AI have pasted company data into chatbot queries, and 22% of those instances involved confidential personal or financial data. In this case, the agent itself, not a human employee, was the vector of data exposure. Because the agent processed external web content as part of its literature review function, it was vulnerable to indirect prompt injection. A threat actor who had been monitoring the company's public research output and publication patterns planted a specifically crafted set of instructions in a preprint paper on a public research repository, anticipating that the agent would process it as part of its literature monitoring workflow.

The injected instruction directed the agent to compile and transmit a summary of recent internal research findings to an external address. The agent, unable to distinguish the malicious instruction from legitimate operational directives in the content it was processing, complied. The exfiltration was not massive in volume, a few hundred pages of synthesized research summary, but it included material from several pre-publication studies that constituted years of proprietary research investment.

The agent's activity logs showed the anomalous outbound transmission, but no one was monitoring them. The agent had been running for nine months without a formal review of its activity, consistent with the OWASP finding that improper offboarding and lack of monitoring are the top non-human identity risk factors. The breach was discovered only when a competitor filed a patent application that included findings closely matching the company's own pre-publication research.

The governance failures stacked: overprivileged access granted for operational convenience, no monitoring of agent activity or output, no validation of the content the agent was ingesting before it was processed as trusted input, no out-of-band confirmation required for the agent to transmit data externally, and no periodic review of the agent's behavior against its expected operational profile. Each of these failures maps directly to a specific control recommended in the governance frameworks examined in Chapter Six: least-privilege access, behavioral monitoring, input validation, output sandboxing, and lifecycle management.

The Cisco State of AI Security 2026 found that only 29% of organizations reported being prepared to secure their agentic AI deployments, with many moving forward with limited readiness, creating exposure across model interfaces, tool integrations, and supply chains. The pharmaceutical case is not atypical. It reflects a gap between the pace of agentic AI adoption and the maturity of governance practices in the substantial majority of organizations currently deploying these systems.

Cross-Case Lessons

Four cases drawn from different sectors, attack types, and outcomes yield a set of lessons that, taken together, constitute a practical checklist for any organization assessing its exposure to the threats this book has mapped.

The first lesson is that the most consequential breaches in this period exploit trust rather than circumventing technical controls. The Bybit heist exploited the trust Bybit placed in Safe's infrastructure. The JLR attack exploited the trust the automotive supply chain places in partner system integrations. The pharmaceutical breach exploited the trust an AI agent placed in the content it was processing. None of these attacks required defeating a firewall or cracking an encryption key. All of them found a trusted path and walked through it.

The second lesson is that detection speed is the variable that mostly determines the magnitude of the outcome. Across financial-sector SOC transformation cases, the difference between a contained incident and a catastrophic one was measured in minutes of dwell time. The JLR production halt lasted five weeks; had the initial compromise been detected in hours rather than days, the supply chain cascade might have been limited to days or not have occurred at all. Speed of detection is the function that AI-powered security improves most reliably, and it is the function where the gap between AI-augmented and traditional security operations is most consequential.

The third lesson is that governance failures are as costly as technical failures. The pharmaceutical case produced competitive harm that no security tool could have prevented after the fact, because the architecture of the agent's deployment created conditions in which the harm was an inevitability rather than a probabilistic risk. The governance investments required to prevent that outcome, least-privilege access, agent monitoring, and input validation, are inexpensive relative to the cost of the breach they prevent.

In a cybersecurity-specific context, adversarial inputs to AI-powered security systems represent a particularly troubling attack vector: the adversary does not need to evade the security system entirely. They need only to craft their malicious activity so that it falls within the distribution of patterns the AI has been trained to classify as benign.- JK. Kojok.

CHAPTER 10
BUILDING YOUR AI-CYBER STRATEGY

There is a reliable pattern in how organizations approach cybersecurity investment: they underinvest until something catastrophic happens, then they overspend reactively on tools that address the specific attack vector that just harmed them, while leaving the next attack vector underprotected. This pattern has been documented across industries for decades. It is expensive, inefficient, and, in the AI era, increasingly untenable.

The pace at which AI is transforming both the threat landscape and the defensive capability of security technology means that organizations that wait for a breach to motivate strategic investment are waiting too long. With the average eCrime breakout time now at twenty-nine minutes and the fastest observed at twenty-seven seconds, the window between initial compromise and significant damage has compressed to the point where reactive investment cannot catch up fast enough to matter in the specific incident that prompted it. The strategy must be built before the attack arrives.

What follows is not a checklist of security products. It is a framework for strategic and governance decisions that determine whether the tools an organization deploys, whatever they are, will actually provide the protection they promise.

Step One: Know What You Have

The foundational prerequisite for any AI-augmented security strategy is inventory, and most organizations have a significant gap between what they believe their inventory contains and what it contains. This gap has three dimensions in the 2026 environment.

The first is traditional asset inventory: the complete population of endpoints, servers, cloud workloads, network devices, and applications that constitute the organization's attack surface. Many organizations have reasonable visibility here, at least for their formally managed assets, though the proliferation of cloud services and shadow IT has significantly expanded the unmanaged perimeter.

The second dimension is the AI inventory: a complete accounting of every AI system, AI tool, and AI agent deployed or used within the organization, whether sanctioned by the security or IT team or not. About 92% of security leaders are concerned about the use of AI agents across the workforce and their impact on security, and sensitive data exposure ranks as their top concern, reflecting awareness that employees are deploying AI tools in ways that create exposure the security team cannot see.

Shadow AI must be discovered before it can be controlled. Machine identity lifecycle management, applying least privilege, credential rotation, monitoring, and governance to every non-human identity, is the foundational priority because you cannot govern what you cannot see. A practical AI inventory addresses: which commercial AI tools employees are using, which AI-powered security products are deployed, which AI agents have been built or acquired for operational functions, what data those agents can access, and which external AI services organizational data is being transmitted to.

The third dimension is the non-human identity inventory described in Chapter Six: the complete population of service accounts, API keys, OAuth tokens, machine certificates, and AI agent credentials that authenticate to organizational systems. Sixty-eight percent of IT security incidents now involve machine identities, and half of the enterprises surveyed have experienced a security breach due to unmanaged non-human identities, making this inventory a security-critical function rather than an administrative one.

Organizations that complete all three inventory dimensions have the foundation for meaningful strategy. Those who skip any one of them are building a strategy on incomplete information, which consistently produces gaps that adversaries will find before the organization does.

Step Two: Assess Your Current Posture Against the AI Threat Taxonomy

One The AI-specific threat taxonomy established in Chapter Four, encompassing prompt injection, data poisoning, model inversion, adversarial inputs, and supply-chain risks in AI components, constitutes a distinct layer of vulnerability that sits atop the conventional cybersecurity risk framework. Most organizations' current security assessments do not explicitly address this layer, leaving even those with mature conventional security postures vulnerable to AI-specific attack techniques.

A practical AI security posture assessment addresses five specific questions.

First, which of your AI systems process untrusted external content? These are the systems most exposed to indirect prompt injection. This is the vulnerability class that the UK National Cyber Security Centre has acknowledged may never be fully mitigated. For each such system, the assessment should document the actions the system can take based on that content and the blast radius if a malicious instruction were executed.

Second, what is the provenance and integrity of your AI training data and fine-tuning datasets? Organizations that have fine-tuned foundation models on proprietary data, or that operate retrieval-augmented generation systems fed by internal knowledge bases, need to assess the integrity of those data sources and the extent to which an adversary could corrupt them and thereby alter the AI system's behavior.

Third, which AI agents have been granted elevated permissions, and are those permissions scoped to the minimum required for the agents' operational functions? High-risk AI operations, including financial transactions, system modifications, and external communications, require explicit human approval because the 2025 attacks discussed earlier demonstrated that configuration-based auto-approval systems can be compromised.

Fourth, are your AI systems covered by your existing security monitoring? The behavioral analytics platforms described in Chapter Three were largely designed and calibrated for human actors and conventional malware. AI agents, which access systems at machine speed, access large volumes, and operate around the clock, produce behavioral profiles that appear anomalous under human-calibrated baselines even when operating normally. They require specific monitoring calibration, and their outputs, not just their access patterns, require validation.

Fifth, have your AI systems been red-teamed for adversarial inputs? Regular adversarial testing is essential because attack techniques evolve rapidly, making yesterday's defenses obsolete today. Organizations should establish ongoing red-team programs specifically focused on AI and agentic AI security. They should treat each successful attack, whether discovered through testing or in production, as intelligence about evolving threat patterns.

Step Three: Adopt AI-Powered Security Tools Strategically

The market for AI-powered security products is large, competitive, and filled with claims that deserve scrutiny. The strategic acquisition of AI security tools follows a different logic from the tactical procurement of point solutions, and organizations that confuse the two consistently end up with fragmented security stacks that provide less protection at a higher cost than a more disciplined architectural approach would have delivered.

The architectural principle that should govern security tool acquisition in 2026 and beyond is platform consolidation over point-solution accumulation. There is a place for AI to augment security in almost every area, from visibility and detection through automated triage and prioritization to autonomous response and advanced forensics. The biggest challenge is navigating beyond the buzzwords to determine which AI tools are right for a given team, how they will integrate into existing workflows, and whether they can find and surface the needle in the haystack.

In practical terms, this means starting with the question of integrated architecture before evaluating specific products. What is the organization's primary threat surface: endpoints, cloud workloads, identity, network traffic, email, or some combination? Where does the most consequential telemetry originate, and where does it currently flow? What security tooling is in place, and what integration work would be required to achieve unified visibility across it? The answers to these questions define the architectural requirements that specific tools must meet.

For organizations that build security capability from a lower baseline, the most impactful initial investments are typically in detection and triage automation, specifically a unified SIEM or XDR platform that can ingest telemetry from existing security tools and apply AI-powered correlation to reduce alert volume to a manageable set of high-confidence actionable events. Organizations deploying AI-augmented SOC platforms consistently report eighty to ninety percent reductions in alert fatigue, sixty percent faster mean time to detect, and fifty percent faster mean time to respond. These improvements are achievable at mid-market scale through managed security service providers that offer AI-powered SOC capabilities as a subscription. This makes the performance differential accessible to organizations that cannot afford to build and staff their own infrastructure.

For organizations with existing, mature security programs, the priority is extending those programs' visibility and governance to cover the AI-specific attack surface: securing AI systems as described in the posture assessment step above, extending identity governance to non-human identities, and adding AI-specific threat intelligence to existing threat-hunting and detection-engineering workflows.

Step Four: Build Governance That Keeps Pace with Deployment

The governance gap documented throughout this book, the distance between the pace at which organizations are deploying AI and the pace at which governance frameworks for those deployments are maturing, is not primarily a technology problem. It is an organizational and leadership problem that requires organizational and leadership solutions. The most effective AI governance frameworks in practice share three characteristics. They are embedded in the deployment process rather than bolted on afterward.

They explicitly define accountability, with named owners responsible for specific governance functions. And they treat governance as a continuous process rather than a one-time assessment.

Embedding governance into deployment means AI systems undergo a security review before going live, not after. The majority of organizations deployed agentic AI in 2025 with limited readiness, creating exposure across model interfaces, tool integrations, and supply chains. The organizations that avoided the consequential governance failures documented in Chapter Nine's pharmaceutical case study were not necessarily more technically sophisticated. They were more disciplined in requiring a security assessment as a precondition for deployment, treating it with the same rigor as for conventional software releases.

In practice, this means that every AI agent deployment goes through a formal access-scoping review that documents the requested permissions, the minimum required permissions, and who is responsible for periodically reviewing those permissions. Every AI system that processes external content has a documented threat model for indirect prompt injection. Every AI system that can take external actions, send emails, execute code, transfer funds, or modify records requires explicit human approval for high-consequence actions, with documented escalation paths when approval is unavailable.

In 2026, compliance frameworks including the EU AI Act, NIST AI RMF, and ISO/IEC 42001 require organizations to maintain three specific compliance deliverables: a control catalog listing each safeguard and how it is enforced at runtime, a compliance matrix mapping controls to regulatory obligations, and a risk register identifying owners, mitigations, and evidence for specific risks including data leakage and unauthorized agent actions. Organizations that build these deliverables as operational infrastructure rather than compliance documentation will find that they also provide the internal visibility required to catch governance failures before they become security incidents.

Step Five: Invest in People, Not Just Tools

The talent dimension of AI cybersecurity strategy is frequently underemphasized in technology-focused discussions, but it is one of the most consequential variables in security outcomes. The World Economic Forum's 2026 Cybersecurity Outlook found that 17% of organizations report insufficient resilience, and 85% of those also lack critical cybersecurity skills, reflecting the structural link between talent and security gaps.

The skills most critically needed are not the same as those that were most critical five years ago. The Tier 1 analyst function, which consisted largely of alert triage and manual log review, is being automated by the AI platforms described in Chapter Three. What organizations need is not more people to perform that function but more people capable of performing the functions that AI cannot: detection engineering, which requires understanding how adversaries actually operate and translating that understanding into detection logic; AI security specialization, which requires both cybersecurity and machine learning knowledge to assess, test, and monitor AI systems for the vulnerability classes described in Chapter Four; and threat intelligence analysis, which requires the contextual judgment to distinguish meaningful signals from noise in the vast information environment of the 2026 threat landscape.

Training existing security professionals in AI security concepts is more immediately achievable than hiring this skill set in a labor market that remains severely supply-constrained. Organizations that invest in structured AI security training for their existing teams, combined with the AI-powered tools that amplify analysts' productivity, will consistently outperform organizations that treat AI security as a specialized function requiring dedicated specialist hires that they cannot attract or afford.

The board and executive dimension of the talent question is equally important. Machine governance is moving from a technical issue to a board-level priority, with executives expected to demonstrate they can audit AI behavior, enforce identity controls, and prove the integrity of AI-driven actions. Organizations whose boards understand the specific risk profile of AI deployment are materially better positioned to make the governance investments that required to close the gaps documented throughout this book than those where AI security is treated as a technical detail beyond executive comprehension.

Step Six: Practice, Measure, and Iterate

Security strategy is not a document produced once and filed. It is a practice sustained continuously against an adversary who is also continuously learning and adapting. The organizations that maintain the best security postures treat security as an operational discipline, not a compliance obligation. The practical expression of this is regular adversarial testing: red team exercises that simulate the specific attack techniques most likely to target the organization, given its sector, geography, and technology profile. Those exercises must explicitly include AI-specific attack scenarios: prompt injection attempts against deployed AI systems, simulated supply chain compromises targeting AI development pipelines, deepfake enabled social engineering against finance and executive teams, and governance-gap exploits that test whether the organization's AI agent controls really hold under adversarial pressure.

To measure security posture requires metrics that reflect the specific outcomes AI-powered security programs aim to produce: mean time to detect, mean time to respond, the ratio of high-confidence alerts to total alerts generated, the percentage of AI agents under continuous behavioral monitoring, and the time elapsed since the last formal review of each AI agent's permissions and behavior against its expected operational profile.

Gartner highlights Continuous Threat Exposure Management as the cornerstone of modern security, emphasizing always-on visibility across identities, endpoints, cloud workloads, and AI systems, with proactive exposure management replacing reactive defense as the primary strategy. The organizations that implement this continuously, not as an annual assessment but as an operational function, are building the adaptive capability required to stay ahead of an adversary that is also operating continuously.

The iterative dimension means treating every incident, whether fully realized or caught early, as an intelligence input that improves the organization's defenses. The pharmaceutical company in Chapter Nine's case study discovered its AI agent breach only when a competitor filed a patent. An organization with functional governance would have discovered it in the monitoring logs and used the near-miss to strengthen its agent oversight. The difference between those two outcomes is not luck. It is the operational discipline of treating security as a learning system rather than a static configuration.

The Strategy in Summary

The organizations that navigate the AI-cybersecurity challenge of 2026 successfully will share a common approach that differs from how most organizations have historically approached security. They will know what they have, including the AI systems and non-human identities that most of their peers are not yet tracking. They will have assessed their specific AI-related exposure, not just their conventional cybersecurity posture. They will have deployed AI-powered defenses at the architectural level rather than piecing together point solutions. They will have built a governance infrastructure that governs AI agents with the same rigor applied to human users. They will have invested in the human capabilities needed to work effectively with AI tools. And they will practice, measure, and iterate continuously, and treat security as a discipline sustained against an adversary rather than a problem solved once.

CHAPTER 11
THE HORIZON

In February 2026, OpenAI CEO Sam Altman confirmed something that security researchers had been tracking with quiet alarm for months: the company's 5.3-Codex model had formally crossed the "High" threshold on OpenAI's internal Preparedness Framework for cybersecurity capability. The designation meant, in plain terms, that the model was assessed as capable of developing working zero-day remote exploits against well-defended systems and of providing meaningful assistance with complex, stealthy intrusion operations.

Security research firm Irregular had documented what it called a "capability shift" in late 2025: frontier AI models had scored near zero on expert-level offensive security challenges until mid-2025, then reached a 60% success rate by that autumn. The trajectory was neither linear nor anticipated. It happened faster than most projections.

The 5.3-Codex threshold crossing was not, by itself, an attack. It was an assessment, conducted under controlled conditions by the company that built the model, aimed precisely at understanding the capability before it could be exploited in the wild. That is the responsible and correct approach. But it is also a data point in a trajectory, and points toward a world that is significantly different from the one this book has been mapping. It points toward a world in which the most sophisticated offensive cyber capabilities are no longer the exclusive province of nation-state intelligence agencies, elite criminal organizations, or specialist security researchers. They are embedded in commercially available AI systems, accessible to anyone with a subscription and sufficient ingenuity to work with them.

Understanding what comes after 2026 requires sitting with that trajectory and following it honestly forward.

The Multi-Agent Battlefield

The agentic AI threat landscape of 2026, documented throughout this book, involves AI agents operating individually within organizational environments, conducting autonomous sequences of action, exploiting identity and permission vulnerabilities, and executing attacks that once required human coordination and teams. What comes next is the multi-agent dimension: swarms of AI agents coordinating with each other to conduct attacks of a complexity and scale that no individual agent, however capable, could execute alone.

Looking beyond 2026, the trajectory of AI in cybersecurity points toward increasingly autonomous and integrated security paradigms, with new attack vectors arising from multi-agent systems and "agent swarms" that require novel security approaches. In the near term, from 2026 to 2028, the weaponization of agentic AI by malicious actors will become more sophisticated, enabling automated reconnaissance and hyper-realistic social engineering at machine speed.

The multi-agent attack architecture mirrors the multi-agent defensive architecture that security vendors are building: specialized agents for reconnaissance, vulnerability exploitation, lateral movement, data exfiltration and laundering, coordinated by an orchestrating agent that assigns tasks, monitors progress, adapts to defensive responses, and ensures that each phase of the attack chain hands off cleanly to the next. As multi-agent systems become prevalent, compromised agents feeding corrupted data to downstream agents can trigger cascading failures in which a single specialized agent's compromise propagates through the entire network of interdependent systems.

Security researchers analyzing the implications of Highly Automated Cyber Capability Agents, or HACCAs, have warned that their faster operational tempo makes inadvertent escalation more difficult to contain. An operation that spreads beyond its intended scope, or that is misinterpreted as targeting nuclear command-and-control infrastructure, could trigger a crisis between nuclear-armed states before anyone has had the opportunity to clarify intent. The most acute risk is that operators lose control of HACCAs once deployed, because design flaws lead to system drift from intended objectives, adversaries find ways to subvert them, or interactions between multiple agents produce effects no one anticipates.

This is not science fiction. The first documented AI-orchestrated cyber-espionage campaign occurred in late 2025. Using commercially available AI software, attackers allegedly automated between 80 and 90 percent of a large-scale cyber espionage campaign targeting approximately 30 organizations worldwide, with human operators involved only in strategic decision-making, such as target selection and data exfiltration approval. The campaign marked the first documented case of an AI-orchestrated cyberattack, representing an escalation from earlier "vibe hacking" operations in which humans directed AI tools rather than delegating orchestration to AI agents. [AUTHOR NOTE: The original text attributed this campaign to "Claude AI software." That attribution requires independent source verification and legal review before publication. Edited to "commercially available AI software" pending confirmation.]

The defensive response to multi-agent attacks requires multi-agent defenses, and the architecture of that response is already under development. IBM's ATOM platform distributes incident response across agents for investigation, threat hunting, identity management, and vulnerability analysis, integrating vendor tools to resolve many incidents within seconds. Simulation-driven approaches, such as Trend Micro's digital twin, enable the coordinated coevolution of red and blue agents in sandboxed environments, improving defensive learning while limiting real-world risk.

The fundamental question that multi-agent cyber conflict raises is one that the security industry is only beginning to grapple with: what does it mean to govern, authorize, and take responsibility for the actions of AI agents that operate faster than human decision-making can keep pace? Effective deployment depends on bounded autonomy: autonomous defense agents can rapidly detect and contain threats, but irreversible actions require explicit authorization boundaries, shared vocabularies, auditable logs, and clear escalation protocols. Designing those boundaries is a governance and engineering challenge that will define the next several years of AI security development. Get them wrong, and you have either deployed autonomous defenders that cannot act fast enough to catch autonomous attackers, or you have deployed autonomous systems that can take irreversible actions without human authorization, which creates a different category of catastrophic risk.

The Quantum Intersection

Quantum computing enters this story not as an imminent crisis but as a slow-building threat that requires action now precisely because it materializes later. The timeline estimates range, but the consensus direction is clear: U.S. government agencies, including NIST and NSA, have issued warnings that Q-Day, the arrival of a cryptographically relevant quantum computer capable of breaking widely used public key encryption, could arrive as early as 2030, particularly if a breakthrough accelerates hardware development. Industry consensus among quantum security experts places the probability of such a computer existing by 2035 at greater than 50%.

The threat that quantum computing poses to cybersecurity is not a future problem. It is a present one, already active, already consequential. The most immediate driver for addressing quantum security today is the 'harvest now, decrypt later' threat model. Adversaries can capture encrypted data today and store it until a sufficiently capable quantum computer enables decryption in the future. As a result, organizations may already be exposed to sensitive information with long-term value, including intellectual property, financial records, government communications, and healthcare data, even in the absence of a visible breach.

Sensitive communications captured in 2026 could be decrypted in 2032. The breach may not be visible when the data is stolen. It becomes visible years later when the encryption protecting it collapses. This is a category of threat with no precedent in the history of cybersecurity: the retroactive breach, in which data believed to be secure at the time of its interception becomes exposed years later through a technological development that was foreseeable but not yet realized.

AI may itself be used to accelerate the development of quantum computing, for example, by developing more efficient error-correction methods, followed by automating the use of quantum power when it arrives. The intersection of powerful quantum capabilities with advanced AI creates scenarios ranging from quantum AGI versus quantum AGI largely canceling each other out, with an asymmetrical advantage to the adversary and a massive advantage to the first mover, to outcomes that most analysis has not yet fully mapped.

NIST finalized its first set of post-quantum cryptographic standards in 2024, providing the algorithmic foundation for the transition. The migration itself is the hard part. The journey to quantum readiness is a massive operational undertaking, made infinitely more complex by a fundamental lack of cryptographic visibility. Most organizations cannot distinguish between which algorithms are simply available in their systems and those actively in use in live sessions. All data stolen today becomes a future liability. And most organizations lack the granular security controls to discover and block the use of outdated, vulnerable ciphers across their infrastructure, making a managed migration nearly impossible to orchestrate without a prior investment in cryptographic inventory.

The migration itself is the hard part, and the difficulty is both technical and organizational. Cryptography is embedded in every layer of the modern technology stack: in the TLS handshakes that secure web traffic, in the certificates that authenticate software updates, in the VPN protocols that protect remote access, in the hardware security modules that guard encryption keys, in the firmware that boots devices, and in the long-lived data archives that organizations have been accumulating for years. Upgrading all these components requires a cryptographic inventory (a complete map of where and how cryptographic algorithms are used across the organization's entire technology estate) that most organizations have never built and cannot build quickly. Without that inventory, migration cannot be planned, prioritized, or executed in any coherent order.

NIST's first post-quantum cryptographic standards, which was finalized in August 2024, selects CRYSTALS-Kyber for key encapsulation and CRYSTALS-Dilithium for digital signatures as the primary standards organizations should migrate toward. The existence of these standards removes one of the major prior barriers to migration: organizations no longer need to wait for algorithmic certainty before beginning transition planning. The remaining barriers are operational: the time and cost required to inventory, test, and upgrade cryptographic dependencies across complex, heterogeneous environments that were never designed for cryptographic agility. Organizations that build that agility now, designing systems to swap cryptographic algorithms without requiring architectural rebuilds, will have an enormous advantage over those that must rebuild from scratch under regulatory pressure when Q-Day arrives.

The organizations that begin cryptographic inventory and post-quantum migration planning now, while quantum computers remain below the threshold of cryptographic relevance, will have years to complete a complex transition in an orderly way. Those who wait for Q-Day to motivate action will find themselves attempting a complex, decade-long migration in crisis conditions, under regulatory pressure, with adversaries who have already accumulated encrypted archives of their most sensitive communications.

The Evolution of Autonomous Defense

Leadership The defensive trajectory mirrors the offensive one: toward greater autonomy, greater speed, and, inevitably, greater delegation of consequential decisions to AI systems that can operate faster than human oversight can follow. Longer-term projections point toward fully autonomous security systems where AI independently defends against threats with minimal human intervention, allowing human experts to transition to strategic management roles. However, as AI proliferates, the attack surface expands, requiring robust governance frameworks that shift from patchwork enforcement to practical operational reality.

The critical design question for autonomous defense is not whether to build systems that can act without explicit human authorization for each action, which is necessary given the speed of AI-powered attacks. It is where to draw the boundaries of what autonomous defensive systems are permitted to do, and how those boundaries are enforced and verified. A defensive AI agent that can autonomously quarantine a compromised endpoint is a significant capability gain over a system that requires analyst approval. A defensive AI agent that can autonomously take an entire network segment offline based on its own threat assessment is a different proposition, with consequences that require different authorization structures.

Current production systems deliberately reflect these constraints: systems that support iterative reasoning and tool use for access control changes, database queries, and code execution remain decision-support systems rather than fully autonomous actors, because the open problem of how to grant execution power without enabling cascading or irreversible failures remains unsolved. The honest assessment of where autonomous defense stands in 2026 is that the capability is ahead of the governance frameworks required to deploy it responsibly at full autonomy. Closing that gap is the central engineering and governance challenge for the next several years.

IBM's ATOM platform, which distributes incident response across specialized agents for investigation, threat hunting, identity management, and vulnerability analysis, represents the current frontier of operationally deployed autonomous defense. Its architecture reveals both the capability and the constraint of the current moment: agents can resolve many incidents within seconds, but consequential actions (those that are irreversible or carry significant operational risk) remain under explicit human authorization. The system is designed to operate at machine speed up to the boundary of human accountability, then pause and escalate. That boundary is precisely designed and carefully maintained. Getting it wrong in either direction leads to failure: too much autonomy produces uncontrolled action, while too little makes the human bottleneck, which is the rate-limiting factor in a machine-speed conflict.

The next several years will be defined by the work of determining where that boundary would be for different categories of action in different organizational contexts, and by the governance and legal frameworks required to hold organizations accountable for the decisions their autonomous systems make. A defensive AI agent that autonomously blocks a network connection is making a security decision. A defensive AI agent that autonomously takes a production system offline is making a business decision with potentially enormous operational consequences. The accountability frameworks for those decisions (who authorizes them, who reviews them, and who bears responsibility when they are wrong) are not yet resolved and resolving them is as important as building the technical capability itself.

Preparing for the Post-Human Operational Tempo

The phrase "post-human operational tempo" does not mean a world without humans in cybersecurity. It means a world in which the pace of cyber conflict has exceeded the pace at which human decision-making can operate as the primary response mechanism. That world is not fully here yet, but the twenty-nine-minute average breakout time documented in 2025, the twenty-seven-second minimum, and the first AI-orchestrated campaigns beginning to appear point directly toward it.

What does preparation look like for that world? It looks like everything in Chapter Ten, implemented with the urgency appropriate to the trajectory: governance infrastructure that governs AI agents before they have been deployed long enough to become entrenched without oversight, cryptographic inventory and post-quantum migration planning that begins this year rather than when Q-Day arrives, autonomous defensive capabilities with authorization frameworks carefully designed before they are deployed rather than retrofitted after an autonomous defensive action causes an unintended consequence, and international coordination on the norms governing autonomous offensive cyber capabilities before a multi-agent attack between nuclear-armed states creates an escalation scenario that no governance framework currently addresses.

As the autonomy and sophistication of agentic systems grow, governance must evolve beyond static compliance to embrace dynamic, lifecycle-aware models of control that include ethical risk forecasting, operational transparency, and shared international norms. The dual-use dilemma remains central: tools originally designed for cyber defense, including autonomous intrusion detection and self-healing systems, can be repurposed for offensive purposes, and the accessibility of these capabilities, combined with the lack of attribution in cyber conflict, creates scenarios where unintended escalation may proliferate.

The horizon is not a cliff edge. It is a gradient, and the organizations, governments, and institutions that begin climbing toward greater AI security maturity now will find themselves on substantially higher ground when the steeper slopes arrive. The technology will continue to accelerate. The threat will continue to evolve. The question that this book has posed from its opening pages, who learns to wield the sword wisely, and how quickly, and with what governance structures guiding their hand, remains the question that will determine the digital security of the coming decade.

The answer is not yet written. But the organizations that understand the trajectory, take the threat seriously without succumbing to fatalism, invest in both technical capability and governance maturity, and treat cybersecurity as the foundational strategic discipline it has become, will be the ones who write it.

CONCLUSION

THE SHARED RESPONSIBILITY

The double-edged sword has been in motion throughout this book's account of 2025- 2026. We have watched it cut through the supply chain of a British automobile manufacturer, disrupting global production for five weeks through a single compromised partner. We have followed it into the Singapore boardroom, where a synthetic CFO authorized a half-million-dollar transfer that never should have been made, and into the Safe wallet platform, where North Korean hackers spent months preparing code that rerouted $1.5 billion in Ethereum in a single eleven-minute window. We have traced its defensive arc too: the eleven minutes in which an AI-powered system detected, investigated, and contained a malware-free intrusion at a European financial firm; the SOC that compressed its mean time to respond from one full day to fourteen minutes; the behavioral analytics that spotted an anomalous vendor credential before any human analyst had seen the first alert.

The sword cuts both ways. That was the promise of the opening chapter, and the evidence for it is now extensive.

But the metaphor contains one more dimension that has been implicit throughout and deserves to be made explicit in closing: a sword requires a hand that knows how to wield it. The technology of AI-powered cybersecurity has matured to the point where capability is no longer the binding constraint. The binding constraint is governance, judgment, and organizational will.

What the Evidence Tells Us

Consider what the evidence shows about the organizations that succeeded in 2026. They are not necessarily the ones with the largest security budgets or most sophisticated technology stacks. They are the ones who treat security as a continuous operational discipline rather than a periodic compliance exercise. They know what AI systems they have deployed, what permissions those systems hold, and what those permissions could do if misused or compromised. They have built governance frameworks that govern AI agents with the same rigor applied to human users. They have extended Zero Trust architecture across every identity (human, machine, and agentic) that touches their systems. They practice incident response before they need it, measure what matters, and treat every near-miss as intelligence about where their defenses need to improve.

These characteristics are not proprietary to large enterprises. They are accessible to organizations at every scale, though the implementations differ. A hospital system with a twelve-person IT team cannot deploy the same AI-powered SOC platform as a global investment bank. But it can maintain an inventory of its AI tools, implement least privilege access for every system account, subscribe to a managed detection service that provides AI-powered monitoring, and require human authorization for any AI-automated action with significant consequences. The principles scale even when the technology implementations do not.

The World Economic Forum's Global Cybersecurity Outlook 2026 makes the equity dimension of this point unmistakable: small organizations are 2.5 times more likely to report insufficient cyber resilience than large enterprises, and the talent shortage is most severe in the regions least equipped to absorb the consequences of a significant breach. The cyber-capable and the cyber-vulnerable are not two separate populations with separate concerns. They are interconnected through supply chains, financial systems, shared infrastructure, and the fundamental interdependence of the global digital economy. A compromised small supplier becomes the entry point for an attack on the large enterprise that depends on it. A breached hospital becomes a vector for attacking the health system around it. The security of the most sophisticated organization in a network is bound by the security of its weakest partner.

A Call to Every Stakeholder

This is why the call to action at the end of this book is not addressed only to CISOs and security teams. It is addressed to every stakeholder in the digital world.

To executives and boards: cybersecurity is no longer a technical issue you can delegate to a team and review at the quarterly risk committee. It is a strategic imperative that requires your direct understanding and active governance. You need to know what AI systems your organization has deployed, what they can access, and what your governance framework for those systems looks like. You need to have practiced your incident response before you need it. And you need to have made the investment decisions (in people, tools, and governance infrastructure) that the threat environment of 2026 demands, not that of five years ago.

To security practitioners: your role is changing faster than your job descriptions reflect. The Tier 1 analyst function is being automated. What the AI era needs from you is what machines cannot provide: contextual judgment, creative adversarial thinking, the ability to reason about novel situations that fall outside any model's training distribution, and the communication skills to translate complex technical realities into organizational decisions. Invest in those capabilities. Invest also in the AI literacy required to work with, audit, and improve the AI systems being deployed alongside you. The analyst who understands how to prompt an AI investigation tool, evaluate its conclusions for completeness and accuracy, and translate its outputs into executive-ready narratives is a fundamentally different and more valuable professional than the analyst who spent a career pattern-matching against SIEM rules.

To governments and policymakers: the regulatory frameworks emerging in 2026 represent genuine progress, but they are racing to keep pace with technology advancing faster than legislation can keep up. The EU AI Act's cybersecurity requirements, the NIST Cyber AI Profile, and the post-quantum cryptography standards are now finalized; these are essential foundations. The gaps that remain, particularly around agentic AI governance, international coordination on state-sponsored AI cyber operations, and the systemic inequity in cyber capability between wealthy and less wealthy nations, require the same seriousness and urgency that was applied to building the frameworks that now exist.

To the security community as a whole: the most consequential defensive asset in 2026 is not any specific technology platform. It is the principle of shared responsibility and collective defense. Threat intelligence sharing, coordinated vulnerability disclosure, collaborative research on AI security techniques, and the open-source community's ongoing work to make capable security tools accessible to organizations without enterprise budgets: all of these reflect an understanding that no single organization, however well-resourced, can secure itself in isolation from the ecosystem around it.

The Choice Ahead

The sword is real. Its edges are sharp. The AI capabilities that have transformed the threat landscape in 2025 and 2026 will not become less capable or less accessible in the years ahead. The multi-agent warfare architectures beginning to emerge, the harvest-now-decrypt-later quantum threat accumulating in data archives worldwide, the agentic systems multiplying across enterprise environments faster than governance frameworks can cover them: all these trajectories point in the same direction. The challenge is escalating, and the required response must also escalate.

But escalation is not the same as inevitability. The organizations documented in this book's case studies that detected threats in eleven minutes, that blocked tens of thousands of attacks in a platform's first year, that built governance structures keeping their AI agents within sanctioned bounds even as adversaries probed for weaknesses: they achieved those outcomes not because they were lucky or uniquely resourced. They achieved them by deliberately and repeatedly choosing to understand the blade.

That is the argument this book has been making from its first page. Not the choice to fear AI, or to ban it, or to pretend the threat is overstated. The choice to understand it: what it can do, what it has already done, what comes next, and what it means to use it wisely in defense of the systems, institutions, and people that depend on the digital world to function.

The sword is already in play. The question, the only question that matters now, is who learns to wield it wisely, and how soon.

GLOSSARY OF KEY TERMS

Below is a comprehensive glossary, covering the key terms, concepts, and technologies introduced throughout the book. Each definition is tailored to the topics explored in the chapters.

Adversarial inputs: Carefully crafted data designed to cause an AI model to produce incorrect, unexpected, or attacker-desired outputs while appearing normal to human observers.

Agentic AI: AI systems designed to pursue goals autonomously, planning sequences of action, using tools, making decisions, and adapting to results without constant human direction. Distinguished from generative AI, which responds to prompts but does not act independently.

Breakout time: The interval between an attacker's initial foothold in a network and their lateral movement to additional high-value systems. The CrowdStrike 2026 Global Threat Report documented an average eCrime breakout time of 29 minutes, with the fastest observed at 27 seconds.

C2PA (Coalition for Content Provenance and Authenticity): An open technical standard for embedding cryptographically signed provenance information into digital media, enabling verification of whether content was captured by a camera, edited by software, or generated by AI.

CRINK: Informal shorthand for China, Russia, Iran, and North Korea: the four nation-states most commonly assessed as posing significant and persistent state-sponsored cyber threats to Western governments and organizations.

Data poisoning: An attack on AI systems in which an adversary corrupts or manipulates training data, causing the resulting model to learn incorrect behaviors or embed hidden backdoors that can be triggered later.

Deepfake: AI-generated synthetic media (video, audio, or images) that realistically depict people saying or doing things they did not actually say or do, produced using generative models trained on real recordings.

EDR (Endpoint Detection and Response): Security software deployed on individual devices that monitors behavior, detects threats, and can automatically contain or respond to incidents at the endpoint level.

HACCA (Highly Automated Cyber Capability Agent): A term used in security research to describe AI agents capable of executing sophisticated, multi-stage cyber operations with minimal human direction, covering reconnaissance through exfiltration.

IAM (Identity and Access Management): The framework of policies, processes, and technologies that govern who (or what) can access which organizational resources, and under what conditions.

LLM (Large Language Model): A type of AI model trained on vast text corpora to predict and generate language. The foundation of systems like ChatGPT, Claude, and Gemini is increasingly embedded in both offensive attack tools and defensive security platforms.

MCP (Model Context Protocol): An open standard developed by Anthropic providing a standardized mechanism for connecting AI systems to external tools, data sources, and services. Rapid adoption in 2025 also expanded the attack surface through malicious or compromised MCP servers.

Model Inversion: An attack in which an adversary systematically queries a deployed AI model to reconstruct or infer the training data used to build it, potentially exposing sensitive personal or proprietary information.

Non-Human Identity (NHI): A digital credential (API key, OAuth token, service account, machine certificate, or AI agent credential) that authenticates a system or automated process rather than a human user. NHIs now outnumber human identities in most enterprises by ratios exceeding 25-to-1.

PQC (Post-Quantum Cryptography): Cryptographic algorithms designed to resist attacks from quantum computers. NIST finalized initial PQC standards in August 2024, including CRYSTALS-Kyber and CRYSTALS-Dilithium.

Prompt injection: An attack in which adversaries embed malicious instructions within content that an AI system processes, causing the system to follow those instructions instead of its legitimate operator's directives. OWASP ranked it as the top vulnerability in LLM applications in 2025.

SOAR (Security Orchestration, Automation, and Response): Technology that automates security incident response workflows, allowing predefined playbooks to execute actions across multiple security tools in response to detected threats.

SOC (Security Operations Center): A centralized team and facility responsible for continuously monitoring an organization's IT environment to detect, analyze, and respond to cybersecurity incidents.

XDR (Extended Detection and Response): A security architecture that ingests and correlates telemetry from multiple security layers (endpoints, networks, cloud workloads, identity systems) into a unified platform, enabling detection of threats that cross domain boundaries.

Zero Trust: A security framework built on the principle of 'never trust, always verify,' requiring continuous authentication and authorization of every user, device, and workload regardless of network location. Being extended in 2026 to govern AI agents and non-human identities alongside human users.

Reference and Resources

The following resources represent the strongest available starting points for readers who want to deepen their engagement with the topics covered in this book. Where possible, each is annotated to explain what it offers and for which audience it is most valuable.

ANNUAL THREAT INTELLIGENCE REPORTS

CrowdStrike Global Threat Report (annual) — The definitive practitioner-facing threat intelligence synthesis, published each February. The 2026 edition introduced the concept of the 'evasive adversary' and documented the first AI-orchestrated espionage campaign. Essential for security professionals. Free download at crowdstrike.com.

World Economic Forum Global Cybersecurity Outlook (annual) — The most comprehensive C-suite and policy-facing synthesis of the cyber risk landscape, produced with Accenture. The 2026 edition covers AI adoption vs. governance gaps, geopolitical fragmentation, and the fraud epidemic. Free at weforum.org.

Darktrace State of AI Cybersecurity (annual) — Based on surveys of 1,500+ security professionals. Provides unparalleled granular insight into how practitioners are actually deploying and experiencing AI security tools. Free at darktrace.com.

IBM X-Force Threat Intelligence Index (annual) — Combines telemetry from IBM's global security operations with research from X-Force. Particularly strong on malware trends, initial access vectors, and critical infrastructure threats. Free at ibm.com/security.

Google Cybersecurity Forecast (annual) — Produced by Google's Threat Intelligence Group (GTIG). Excellent on nation-state actor trends, AI misuse in attack campaigns, and ICS/OT risks. Free at cloud.google.com.

NIST STANDARDS AND FRAMEWORKS

NIST AI Risk Management Framework (AI RMF 1.0) — The foundational US government framework for identifying, assessing, and managing AI-specific risks. Governs AI procurement for federal agencies; widely adopted in regulated industries. Free at nist.gov.

NIST AI 100-2: Adversarial Machine Learning Taxonomy — The authoritative technical taxonomy of AI-specific attack types: evasion, poisoning, privacy, and abuse attacks. Essential reading for any security practitioner working with AI systems. Free at nvlpubs.nist.gov.

NIST Cybersecurity Framework 2.0 (CSF 2.0) — Updated 2024 edition of the framework that underpins most enterprise security programs. The developing Cyber AI Profile extends CSF 2.0 to AI-specific risks. Free at nist.gov.

NIST Post-Quantum Cryptography Standards (FIPS 203/204) — The finalized standards for quantum-resistant cryptographic algorithms. Mandatory reading for any organization beginning PQC migration planning. Free at nist.gov.

BOOKS

The Cuckoo's Egg by Cliff Stoll (1989) — The original true-crime cybersecurity narrative, following the first documented nation-state cyber espionage operation. Still the best introduction to how intrusions actually unfold, and to the cat-and-mouse dynamics that have defined the field since its beginning.

Sandworm by Andy Greenberg (2019) — The definitive account of Russia's Sandworm hacking unit and its NotPetya attack — the most destructive cyberattack in history. Essential context for understanding why nation-state cyber operations have cascading collateral effects far beyond their intended targets.

This Is How They Tell Me the World Ends by Nicole Perlroth (2021) — A sweeping investigation into the global zero-day vulnerability market. Provides the best available public account of how nation-state offensive cyber capabilities are acquired, traded, and deployed.